The Lexicon

The Lexicon

WILLIAM F. BUCKLEY JR.

ILLUSTRATED BY Arnold Roth

Introduction by Jesse Sheidlower

A Harvest Original

Harcourt Brace & Company

San Diego   New York   London

Published by arrangement with Random House, Inc.

Library of Congress Cataloging-in-Publication Data
Buckley, William F. (William Frank), 1925–
[Buckley lexicon]
The lexicon / William F. Buckley Jr.: illustrated by Arnold Roth:
introduction by Jesse Sheidlower.—1st Harvest ed.
p.   cm.
Originally appeared in Buckley, the right word under the title:
A Buckley lexicon.
"A Harvest original."
ISBN 0-15-600616-2
1. English language—Glossaries, vocabularies, etc. 2. English
language—Terms and phrases. 3. Vocabulary.   I. Title.
PE1689.B77   1998
428.1—dc21   98-21622

Designed by Lydia D'moch

Printed in the United States of America
First Harvest edition 1998
A C E F D B

Contents

Introduction

THE FIRST TIME I met William F. Buckley we were both members of a televised panel discussing words. The moderator, introducing me with a pop quiz to test my credentials, asked me to define the word *usufruct*. I felt smug as I recited, "The right to enjoy another's property as long as you don't damage it." Then Mr. Buckley leaned into his microphone and quoted an entire paragraph on *usufruct* from the political economist Henry George.

We have any number of authors who revel in arcane vocabulary, but Mr. Buckley surpasses them all, for the simple reason that when he uses a hard word, *He knows what it means.* Anyone can open a big dictionary and find thousands—nay, tens or hundreds of thousands—of words that no one knows and hardly anyone has ever used. And the continuing popularity of hard-word books, newspaper quizzes, and the like demonstrates that many people find such words fascinating. I will admit to a certain *frisson of joy* whenever I come across a rare word and I get the opportunity to include it in my files. But let's be honest: Who cares about the word for the fear of having peanut butter stick to the roof of your mouth? (Mr. Buckley pointedly does *not* care that this word is *arachibutyrophobia,* and he follows the critic Dwight Macdonald in condemning it and its ilk to the "zoo section" of dictionaries.)

No, what makes Mr. Buckley distinctive is that he, unlike most of the hard-word crowd, genuinely uses these words, and he uses them because they fit what he wants to say. He uses them in context, without calling special attention to them, because he knows them, not because he scribbled them in a notebook after finding them in the *Oxford English Dictionary.* He uses them because they are right.

The Lexicon is a monument to his distinctiveness.

What lexicographers value above all else is a good citation for a word. A citation is an example of a word used in context, and that context is all-important. The sentence "The word for the fear of having peanut butter stick to the roof of your mouth is *arachibuty-rophobia,*" for example, is an extremely poor citation (though it's likely to be the only context in which you'll ever find this word, which is telling in itself). On the other hand, Mr. Buckley's sentence "We face a concrete problem in Europe given the tergiversation of Helmut Kohl on the modernizing of the remaining nuclear missiles in West Germany" is an excellent citation, since it shows that *tergiversation*—which means "the reversal of one's opinions; backsliding" and comes from a Latin word meaning "to turn one's back"—is a word still in use; in fact, it appeared in a widely read syndicated column.

Every word in *The Lexicon,* from *abattoir* to *xenophobia,* comes complete with a citation showing you exactly how Mr. Buckley has used it. *The Lexicon* is the *Oxford English Dictionary* of William F. Buckley. And like the *OED,* what is most important is not the definitions (though these, Mr. Buckley's own, are excellent), nor the size (despite its twenty volumes, the *OED* has some 200,000 fewer entries than *Webster's Second*), but rather the citations, which allow us to read along with one of the greats and see how a master works his craft.

We can see such inkhorn words as *eructation,* "a violent belching out or emitting"; *williwaw,* "a gust of cold wind"; *machicolation,* "an opening for shooting or dropping missiles upon assailants attacking below"; *phlogistonic,* "heat-producing"; *lucubrate,* "to discourse learnedly in writing" (a favorite word of Byron); and *unmeeching,* "not cringing, sneaky, or whining in tone."

We can also see a selection of words that are in many people's passive vocabulary, that is, the words that one probably knows but rarely uses, such as *didactic,* "characteristic of the teacher"; *recondite,* "very difficult to understand"; *taciturn,* "temperamentally disinclined or reluctant to talk or converse"; *probity,* "uncompromising adherence to the highest principles and ideals"; *adumbrate,* "to outline broadly."

While anyone reading through this book will arrive at a personal favorite (mine is *eristic,* "finely argumentative"), it is likely that Mr. Buckley would discourage a single choice in favor of the sort of broad knowledge that allows him to choose *usufruct* because he reads Henry George, not because he reads *Mrs. Byrne's Dictionary of Unusual, Obscure, and Preposterous Words.*

Robert W. Burchfield, the former chief editor of the Oxford English dictionaries, tells of overhearing a cocktail-party guest asking, "Why does Anita Brookner use hard words like 'rebarbative' and 'nugatory'?" Dr. Burchfield opines, "One possible answer is that the famous novelist does not regard them as 'hard.'" As Mr. Buckley has pointed out in one of his many defenses of his vocabulary choices, "We tend to believe that a word is unfamiliar because it is unfamiliar to us." We must be grateful to Mr. Buckley, for it is a splendid introduction to the world of words that is rich but will no longer be strange.

—*Jesse Sheidlower*

A

abattoir (noun) *Slaughterhouse.*

I wondered amusedly and intensively, what could J. K. Galbraith be up to, revealing these thoughts as we approached the **abattoir,** the Cambridge Union?

aberrant (noun) *A person whose behavior departs substantially from the standards for behavior in his group.*

It is not unlikely that this book, upon its appearance, will be branded as the product of an **aberrant** who takes the Wrong Side, i.e., the side that disagrees with the "liberals."

aberration (noun) *Deviation from the truth or a moral standard, from the natural state, or from a normal type.*

Now Jeane Kirkpatrick is my sister and Pat Buchanan my brother, and if I have ever differed from their foreign policy analyses it can only have been in a moment of **aberration.**

ab initio (adverb; Lat.) *From the beginning.*

He had begun Latin, last year, at Greyburn, and had been trained *ab initio* in the English sequence.

abjure (verb) *To disclaim formally or disclaim upon oath.*

An insurrectionary movement, it is dominated by men committed to Communist doctrine and methods who refused to **abjure** the use of force and terrorism to achieve their goals.

ablutions (noun) *The washing of one's body or part of it.*

Several witnesses noted the license number, and the California authorities had it within minutes, leaving it a mystery why there was no one there at his apartment to greet Edgar Smith when he drove in to perform the identical **ablutions** of nineteen years earlier—an effort to remove the blood from his person and clothing.

abominate (verb) *To loathe; detest.*

I had never heard of the gentleman, a professor of English from the University of Missouri, who wrote a review of *Saving the Queen* for the *Kansas City Star*. He made it quite clear that he had spent a considerable part of his adult life **abominating** me and my works and my opinions. He was manifestly distressed at not quite disliking my first novel.

abortifacient (noun) *A drug or any agent that induces abortion.*

The Choicers are now saying that the Griswold decision must be understood as permitting not merely physical barriers to impregnation, but also **abortifacients.**

abrogate (verb) *To rescind; abolish by official action.*

It would be quite mistaken to **abrogate** the treaty in reaction to these infractions: Nothing would more quickly propel the three quarters of the Panamanian community that dislikes Noriega to return to his fold.

absolutized (verb) *Made absolute; converted to an absolute.*

Joyce's *Ulysses* was okayed by a federal court after a long struggle, and pretty soon so was *Lady Chatterley's Lover*, and since then, such a book as *American Psycho*, the First Amendment having been **absolutized** in its application.

abstruse (adjective) *Difficult to understand, to penetrate the meaning of.*

Here is a man [Cardinal Arns of São Paulo] who studied literature at the Sorbonne, where he achieved his doctorate; who taught patrology and didactics at highly respected universities; who has written twenty-five books, including **abstruse** treatises on medieval literature.

accelerability (noun) *The capacity to speed up; potential for quickening.*

The **accelerability** of economic development by force of will (a premise of the Point Four Program) is an article of faith for leading liberal spokesmen.

accession (noun) *Something added, as to a collection or formal group.*

Abbie Hoffman is not the King of England, but the point of course is that he seeks a kind of metaphorical **accession** to the throne by the use of any means.

accretion (noun) *Something that has been added that doesn't necessarily belong.*

The minimum wage is an **accretion** of the New Deal that is not publicly defended by any serious economist.

acerbic (adjective) *Sharply or bitingly ironic.*

His only apparent extracurricular involvements were an occasional letter to the *Yale Daily News,* **acerbic,** polished, and conclusive in the sense of unfailingly suggesting that any contrary opinion should not presume to expect from him any rebuttal.

acidulous (adjective) *Biting, caustic, harsh.*

By May 14, 1981, Edgar Smith had become, in the **acidulous** words used by one commentator, "the most honored murderer of his generation."

acumen (noun) *Acuteness of mind; keenness of perception; discernment or discrimination.*

I bet his students did, all right—if they called Mr. Root a fascist-by-association, they might well have earned a reward for showing high critical **acumen.**

adamantine (adjective) *Unyielding, inflexible.*

He gave the relevant details of the life of Bertram Heath. He stressed the central role of Alistair Fleetwood as the formative influence in Bertram Heath's life. He underlined the **adamantine** refusal of Fleetwood to any interview concerning Bertram Heath.

adducing (verb) *Bringing forward as an example, reason, proof, for consideration in a discussion, analysis, or contention; offering, presenting, citing.*

How mischievous is the habit of **adducing** reasons behind everything that is done! I can unassailably delight in lobster and despise crabmeat so long as I refrain from giving reasons.

ad hominem (adjective; Lat.) *Marked by an attack on an opponent's character rather than by answer to his contention.*

Beame was so clearly above that kind of suspicion that an insinuation to that effect was never even raised, not even in a campaign desperate for issues and gluttonous for ***ad hominem*** argument.

adjudication (noun) *A formal ruling by a tribunal.*

So how do we make the final **adjudication?** Why not use a Democratic measurement of the Misery Index? Under Mr. Carter, the Misery Index stood at 19.8. Under Mr. Reagan, at this moment, it is 15.8.

ad libitum (adverb; Lat.) *In accordance with one's wishes; ad lib.*

To have proposed abortions ***ad libitum*** was, quite simply, unthinkable for a politician.

ad rem (adjective; Lat.) *Pertinent to the matter or person at issue; directed at the specific thing.*

Ad rem depersonalizations are necessary to social life, and are not any more inhumane intrinsically than the motions of the mother counting noses before deciding how much dinner to cook.

adulator (noun) *One who praises effusively and slavishly, flatters excessively, fawns upon.*

Edward Bennett Williams introduced to the jury a man who happens to be a Communist Party-liner in international affairs and an **adulator** of Nikita Khrushchev.

adumbrate (verb) *To foreshadow, symbolize, or prefigure in a not altogether conclusive or not immediately evident way; to give a sketchy representation of; to outline broadly, omitting details.*

What Richard Rovere resists so fiercely, for reasons he has not thought through, is the insinuation that what one might call the Liberal Establishment holds to a definable orthodoxy (his going on to **adumbrate** that orthodoxy was sheer brinksmanship).

adventitious (adjective) *Coming from another source; added or appended extrinsically and not sharing original, essential, or intrinsic nature.*

You cannot accomplish the elimination of twenty-five million Xs by so simple an arrangement as multiplying by twenty-five million the **adventitious** elimination of a single X, effected in spontaneous circumstances.

aegis (noun) *The direction, control, supervision.*

The key to stopping the erosion of Eastern's assets under the **aegis** of the judge who seems to have the power to conduct either an autopsy or a revivification is, of course, the unions.

Aesopian (adjective) *Conveying an innocent meaning to an outsider but a concealed meaning to an informed member of a conspiracy or underground movement.*

A great deal depends on the question whether Saddam Hussein can think straight, because much of what has come from him, and goes out to him, is rendered in the **Aesopian** mode: stuff that says one thing but implies or seeks to imply another.

affect (verb) *To pretend; to give the impression of; to feign.*

When Larry Fillmore told his superior in the Agency that he had become engaged, he was told that on no account could he reveal to his fiancée what his actual affiliation was, that he must continue to **affect** to be a Foreign Service trainee.

affectation (noun) *A manner of speech or behavior not natural to one's actual personality or capabilities.*

He had intended to ask Anthony whether "10:36" was an **affectation**, but forgot, and accordingly took pains to be punctual.

afflatus (noun) *A creative impulse; a divine warrant or inspiration.*

As Muhammad Ali explained, "I was the onliest boxer in history people asked questions like a senator." But then he was touched by the **afflatus** of Elijah Mohammed.

a fortiori (adverb; Lat.) *All the more convincingly; with greater reason; with still more convincing force.*

A mother, while obviously exercising *de facto* authority over the survival of the fetus, is nevertheless legally and *a fortiori* morally nothing more than the custodian of the fetus whose insulation against abuse ought to be guaranteed by the state.

agglomeration (noun) *An indiscriminately formed mass.*

Yale's mission is not articulate except insofar as an **agglomeration** of words about enlightened thought and action, freedom and democracy, serve to define the mission of Yale.

agglutinate (verb) *To unite or combine into a group or mass.*

The clerk uttered the workaday incantation in the humdrum cadences of the professional waterboy at court. The procedure is everywhere the same. The speed must be routinized, and accelerated, like liturgical responses, the phrases **agglutinated,** yet somehow audible.

aggrandize (verb) *To make great or greater, as in power, honor, or wealth.*

We turned over to their Communist oppressors tens of millions not only by defaulting on our moral obligations and diminishing our identification with justice, but also by **aggrandizing** greatly the enemy's power.

agnosticism (noun) *The doctrine that the existence or nature of any ultimate reality is unknown and probably unknowable or that any knowledge about matters of ultimate concern is impossible or improbable.*

The rhetorical impulses of the day are sluggish in the extreme; they place an immoderate emphasis on moderation, and promote a philosophical gentility, deriving from **agnosticism,** that permeates our moral intellectual life to its distinct disadvantage.

albescent (adjective) *Becoming white, i.e., shining out more conspicuously.*

Nobody knows how Congress is going to leave Social Security and the other entitlement programs untouched and come up with $50 billion or so to save the savings and loans, which we are informed need to be saved because the alternative—letting them fail—is more costly in the long run because Congress has insured the depositors against harm. And there is the **albescent** matter of a United States with (a) no nuclear weapons facilities, and (b) a lot of unmanageable toxic nuclear waste material.

allurement (noun) *Something that attracts or entices.*

A great arsenal of rights and perquisites and **allurements** and toys has been organized for the benefit of youth, and it has been questioned whether it does young people the good Americans wish for them to continue in the direction we have taken with respect to their growing years.

altruistic (adjective) *Pertaining to a disinterested consideration of, regard for, or devotion to others' interests.*

It could in fairness be said that all the money thus solicited goes straight to the student in one form or another. In the last analysis, it is being solicited for **altruistic** purposes.

ambient (adjective) *Surrounding on all sides; encompassing, enveloping.*

Here are some **ambient** data by which we gain perspective. It costs $35,000 per year to maintain a soldier in the army. It costs $30,000 per year to keep an inmate in jail. It costs $13,000 per year for each VISTA volunteer. It costs $20,000 per student for four years of ROTC.

ameliorate (verb) *To improve; make better.*

To suggest that politics is not the solution is to endanger political careers. It is not a subject directly addressed by Jean-François Revel—the difficulty in achieving the desired circulation of thought, for the purpose of **ameliorating** such problems as race relations in such a country as the United States.

amenities (noun) *Social courtesies; pleasantries; civilities.*

They didn't exchange even routine goodbyes. The Director and his principal spymaster were not, really, friends. When there were **amenities** exchanged they tended to be formalistic.

amorphous (adjective) *Without clearly drawn limits; not precisely indicated or established; without definite nature or character; not allowing clear classification or analysis.*

The National Center for Policy Analysis, based in Dallas, has issued a report called "Tax Fairness: Myths and Reality"... which is as lucid and pointed as Goreism is convoluted and **amorphous.**

amulet (noun) *Charm often inscribed with a spell, magic incantation, or symbol and believed to protect the wearer against evil.*

The President should be given a line-item veto, sure, but those who think the budget deficit is as easy to solve as by giving the Chief Executive this **amulet** will have to think again.

analogue (noun) *Something similar; another version of the same thing.*

They speak of Sen. Joseph McCarthy paralyzing the Foreign Service: Will history give us any **analogue** more indicative of the power of superstition than that of the anti-nuclear lobbyists over the development of nuclear power?

anarchic (adjective) *Tending toward anarchy; lawless, rebellious.*

The policeman was relieved when the young man suddenly strode off, because his build, though slim, was pronouncedly athletic, and deep in his eyes there was an **anarchic** stubbornness, which policemen detailed to guarding the Soviet legation were experienced enough to spot.

anathema (noun) *A vigorous denunciation.*

I ask reasonable observers to look out for evasive and irrelevant answers, for rebuttal by epithet, for flowery **anathemas.**

Anglophilia (noun) *A particularly unreasoned admiration of or partiality for England or English ways.*

Helen had long since become accustomed to Blackford's desire to meet everyone, which she attributed to natural gregariousness, and a galloping **Anglophilia.**

anfractuous (adjective) *Full of twists and turns; winding; tortuous.*

Alistair Fleetwood had several reactions to what he had been told. Triumph, clearly: Unless he had drastically misunderstood the **anfractuous** message of Alice Goodyear Corbett, the Great God Beria had backed down and agreed to see him.

angst (noun) *A kind of perpetual, even neurotic state of anxiety.*

One artist sought to explain his **angst** by sticking a crucifix in a jar of urine. That this exhibit should be financed by taxpayers is a proposition Senator Helms had no difficulty taking on.

animadversion (noun) *An unfriendly reference, statement, criticism.*

The machinists of Eastern Airlines tend to slur off into **animadversions** on the management of Frank Lorenzo, whose personality poses no threat to Perry Como's.

animadvert (verb) *To remark or comment critically, usually with strong disapproval or censure.*

John Kenneth Galbraith asked me just when major corporations had lost 85 percent of their value: and I evaded an answer (I did not have the data in the front of my memory; and in any event, I had exaggerated the effect of the Dow Jones dip of 1969–70 by **animadverting** one of JKG's books, suggesting that its collapse had coincided with that of the market). Manifestly, I did not get away with this, and ought not to have done.

animus (noun) *Ill will, antagonism, or hostility, usually controlled, but deep-seated and sometimes virulent.*

The anti-American **animus** was not really all that transparent until just

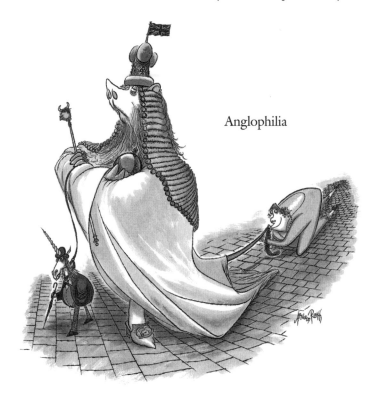

Anglophilia

before the punishment began, and on through the ferocity of it and the hideously redundant final blows.

anneal (verb) *To strengthen; toughen.*

The myth of Napoleon suffered mortal wounds. It required three more years to put him away permanently, but the resolve to do so was **annealed.** This time they'll probably award Gorbachev not a lifetime on St. Helena, but a Nobel Peace Prize. Machiavelli can be taken too far.

anomalous (adjective) *Unusual in context; abnormal.*

A U-2 flight, doing its twice-a-week run over Cuba, had yielded an **anomalous** picture taken over San Cristóbal.

anomaly (noun) *Deviation from the normal or common order, form, or rule; abnormality.*

The "conservatives" in the Kremlin are those who desire a return of Stalinism. Sometimes the **anomalies** bite back. *The New York Times* ran a sober account from Moscow about a crackdown by "Kremlin conservatives" against the importation of foreign books. One of the proscribed titles was *The Conscience of a Conservative* by Barry Goldwater.

anomie (noun) *A state of rootlessness in which normative standards of conduct and belief have weakened or disappeared; a similar condition in an individual, commonly characterized by personal disorientation, anxiety, and social isolation.*

Edgar Smith had walked out of Trenton into the more incapacitating bonds of **anomie.**

anthropomorphize (verb) *To attribute a human form or personality to forces or things greater than human.*

But it's also true that his was a critical as well as a symbolic (and telegenic) role, and that the American habit is to **anthropomorphize**— Napoleon, not his footsoldiers, is lionized.

antimacassar (noun) *A cover thrown over the backs or arms of chairs to protect them from Macassar hair oil or other soilage; thus, tidily, fussily old-fashioned.*

To the argument that in combat conditions it is a burden to provide two sets of washroom facilities, the pleaders for what they call women's rights argue to the effect that in combat situations, **antimacassar** niceties become simply irrelevant, and that, after all, even in the narrow confines of a foxhole, it is possible to make token adjustments.

antinomian (adjective) *Opposed to, defiant of, or rejecting moral law.*

William Kunstler was probably the best-known of the lawyers who identified themselves with dissent, and who sought a kind of **antinomian** liberty for dissenters.

antipodal (adjective) *Opposed; widely different.*

More academic and philosophical attention has been devoted in the last fifty years to the flowering of Marxist thought and life under Marxism. Still, it is astonishing how little thought is given to the great residual paradox expressed in the **antipodal** manifestos of our time.

antiquarian (adjective) *Of or belonging to the antiquities, the study of antiquities, or old times.*

The direction we must travel requires a broadmindedness that strikes us as **antiquarian** and callous.

aperçu (noun; Fr.) *A brief glimpse or immediate impression, especially an intuitive insight.*

Professor Edward Luttwak came up several years ago with a hauntingly bright *aperçu* calculated to distinguish between Mao man and Soviet man.

aphoristic (adjective) *Characterized by concise, artful, quotable statements or principles; terse and often ingenious formulations of truth or sentiment.*

As it happens, the camera in Hanover is zooming in on a disaffected young staffer, a Chinese-American who had twice been reprimanded by the staff of *The Dartmouth Review* for seeking to insert bawdy quotations into the page given over to reproducing **aphoristic** or amusing quotes.

apodictically (adverb) *Expressing necessary truth; with absolute certainty.*

The prediction (mine) that the two major candidates would differ from one another only in the appoggiaturas was, it turned out, correct. The *New York Times* made the point **apodictically**.

apogee (noun) *The farthest or highest point.*

Clive Bell observed that the grandeur and nobility of the Allied cause during World War I "swelled in ever vaster proportions every time it was restated"—reaching its **apogee** in our explicitly formulated determination to make the world safe for democracy.

apostasy (noun) *Defection from one's faith, political or religious.*

I was left to infer that while serving as a courier, Whittaker Chambers was proving to his case officer his utter reliability (subject, of course, to apostasy from the Communist movement).

a posteriori (adjective; Lat.) *Arriving at a principled conclusion as a result of an examination of the facts; reasoning from the particular to the generality.*

Will the historians trained in *a posteriori* sleuthing say to us one day, "Kennedy got this insight from the history of Walpole that Galbraith gave him to read"? Did JFK read it?

appoggiatura (noun; It.) *An accessory embellishing note or notes preceding an essential melodic note or tone.*

He knew not to expect any explanation of how the mission had been accomplished—these romantic *appoggiaturas* on the mechanics of the spy business were peculiarly the anxiety of the Americans and the British.

apriorism (noun) *Reasoning from principles to particulars; thus, if free speech is right, the person who exercises it is right.*

Nothing is more futile—or, for that matter, more anticonservative—than to indulge the heresy of extreme **apriorism.**

arbiter elegantiae (noun; Lat.) *The person who rules on matters of fashion, protocol, taste.*

Professor Arthur Schlesinger, who is the *arbiter elegantiae* of liberal fashion, wrote a few months ago that only bigots would vote against Jesse Jackson.

arcana (noun) *Secret or mysterious knowledge or information known only to the initiate.*

Truman Capote was something of a lay criminologist, appearing on talk shows, explaining such terms as "sociopath," "psychopath," and other **arcana** of penological psychology.

arcane (adjective) *Very unusual; the kind of thing generally known only to scholars.*

There were some difficulties, mostly revolving about Spanish translations for **arcane** Russian terminology. Happily most nuclear language relies heavily on Greek and Latin roots and it never proved impossible finally to communicate everything Pushkin wanted to communicate.

arrant (adjective) *Naked, unmitigated.*

Soviet television is showing only pictures of Chinese students attacking Chinese soldiers. And the Soviet press quote only Chinese officials' statements in which the student protesters emerge as "counterrevolutionaries" guilty of sadistic killing of patriotic soldiers.

Any excuses for this kind of behavior are **arrant** Bolshevism of the old school.

arrogation (noun) *To claim or seize without right; appropriate to oneself arrogantly; ascribe or attribute without reason.*

In the long view of it, conservatives have tended to be suspicious of the **arrogation** of power by the Executive.

arterial (adjective) *Of or designating a route of transportation carrying a main flow with many branches.*

The street outside was a heavily used **arterial** road running into London.

artifact (noun) *A usually simple object showing human workmanship or modification, as distinguished from a natural object.*

It is encouraging when Professor Galbraith is struck rather by his craftsmanship than by the **artifact.** Michelangelo would have been entitled to admire anything he had sculpted, even gallows.

artifice (noun) *A wily or artful stratagem; guile.*

Oakes flushed, doodling on his pad, conscious that everyone was looking at him, unlearned in the **artifices** of appearing indifferent.

ascetic (adjective) *Disposed to do without luxuries; austere.*

Faith Partridge was an **ascetic** woman, in part by nature, in part by necessity; she needed to hold together a household headed by a free-lance writer whose work was mostly rejected, which rejections drove him to despondent drink, even as his occasional acceptances drove him to festive drink.

asceticism (noun) *Rigorous self-discipline, severe abstinence, austerity.*

Bauhaus was the name given to a compound of architects gathered together after the First World War in Germany to remark the general desolation, which they sought to shrive by a kind of architectural **asceticism** noted for a cleanness of line, an absence of ornamentation, the blandness of color, and the "honesty" of generic building materials.

asperity (noun) *Roughness of manner or temper.*

Brother Hildred asked "Leo" if he would like to visit the school's physics laboratory that afternoon. Tucker replied that he would not like to visit it this afternoon, tomorrow, next month, or next year. But quickly he recoiled from his apparent **asperity,** and simply said he did not wish to revisit any aspect of his past professional life.

aspersion (noun) *The act of calumniating; defamation.*

I mention Robert Kennedy without **aspersion** of any kind—on the contrary; because his foes and his friends agree that he felt deeply, and it is at least the public understanding that he was not merely a practicing Catholic but a believing Christian.

aspirant (noun) *One who is ambitious of advancement or attainment.*

Quite possibly the **aspirant** mayor, in order to get himself elected, would need to make precisely those commitments to the old order which preclude the very actions needed to overcome those crises.

asseveration (noun) *An assertion made in very positive form; a solemn assertion.*

Dr. Robert DuPont gave the impression that he had disposed of any question (as to whether drugs ought to be legalized) before the house by his initial **asseveration.** To wit, "Name me one politician in the United States who has run successfully for political office who believes in legalizing drugs."

asseveratively (adverb) *With positive or emphatic affirmation.*

I am going to devote my time today to setting forth one or two propositions, some of which I tender **asseveratively,** others—well, inquisitively.

assiduously (adverb) *Marked by constant, unremitting attention or by persistent, energetic application.*

Robert Price resisted, his contention being that Lindsay's candidacy was best served by flatly ignoring his Conservative opponent, which Lindsay proceeded **assiduously** to do.

assonant (adjective) *Marked by resemblance of sound in words or syllables; resemblance.*

In Garry Trudeau's "Doonesbury," the reader is well nourished, all the more so since there is all that wonderful **assonant** humor and derision in midstrip: indeed, not infrequently the true climaxes come in the penultimate panel, and the rest is lagniappe.

asymptotically (adverb) *Getting closer and closer to a goal, but never quite reaching it.*

The ceremony reaches cyclical heights of debauchery every few years as the management struggles, **asymptotically,** towards the goal of fully anesthetizing the losers' pain.

atavistic (adjective) *The reappearance, after a considerable interval, of an organism or cultural habit.*

When it becomes self-evident that biological, intellectual, cultural, and psychic similarities among races render social separation capricious and **atavistic,** then the myths will begin to fade, as they have done in respect of the Irish, the Italians, the Jews.

athwart (preposition) *Across; from one side to another; against; in opposition to.*

Sometimes one is tempted to take a bucketful of that clayey mud resembling creamy peanut butter and drip it over the heads of the Luddite lobby that stands **athwart** progress yelling Stop!

atomistic (adjective) *An object or concept viewed as particles of the whole.*

I do not believe it is undignified to confess to having been critically influenced by a teacher, or a faculty, or a book; but the accent these days is so strong on **atomistic** intellectual independence that to suggest such a thing is highly inflammatory.

attenuate (verb) *To stretch out; prolong.*

That was the rumor that caught Cubela's attention and that led, after two months' excruciatingly **attenuated** probing of contacts, to the first communication between Rolando Cubela and Rufus.

Attican (adjective) *Athenian in its classical simplicity, elegance.*

We should all be in favor of short speeches. But if we're going to set up an **Attican** theatrical background to commemorate the moment of the Soviet departure from Afghanistan, why doesn't General Gromov use up his one minute and seven seconds to fire a bullet into his head?

aught (noun) *Nothing; zero; cipher.*

One irrepressible senior, who did not care **aught** for ideology, but was bent on cashing in on those political impulses, announced that after graduation he would launch a firm to take over the foreign policy of sovereign states.

augur (verb) *To predict or foretell, especially from signs or omens.*

Every delegate found a copy of that letter under his door the next morning; this generated wild rumors, huge resentments, a divided convention, a divided Republican Party, and **augured** a defeat in November.

auspices (noun) *The umbrella under which you operate; the patronage.*

No questions. No nothing. But perhaps all that would happen in Havana? Indeed it did, although the **auspices** were unexpected.

auto-da-fé (noun; Port.) *The ritual accompanying the execution of a heretic, used especially in connection with the Inquisition.*

Here was a modern *auto-da-fé*: not for countenancing heresy, but for denouncing it.

avatar (noun) *A high priest; a semi-god; an incarnate authority.*

There was talk by the **avatars** of a free press charging cowardice and betrayal of common responsibilities to defend the First Amendment.

avuncular (adjective) *The kind of thing you'd expect of an uncle; benevolent.*

"I was class of 1918." He smiled his warm, **avuncular** smile. "It's hard for old fogies like me to think of women at Yale, though I know they've always been in the graduate school."

B

badinage (noun) *Light conversation; banter.*

Anthony said something or other, lapsing into **badinage,** and they signed off.

banal (adjective) *Lacking originality, freshness, or novelty; failing to stimulate, appeal, or arrest attention.*

He begins to recount his misgivings about American society, the war, the draft, the profit system, the educational establishment. My answers are diffuse, **banal,** and repetitious.

banality (noun) *Something obvious; repetitious; lacking in originality.*

In Warsaw President Bush told the press, "There are times in diplomacy when a certain delicacy is called for." Putting that on the front page of *The New York Times* could have been the work of a sly reporter whose only defense against **banality** is to print it.

banausic (adjective) *Of purely mechanical interest or purpose.*

Al Lowenstein was the original activist, such was his impatience with the sluggishness of justice, so that his rhythms were more often than not disharmonious with those that govern the practical, **banausic** councils of this world.

bawdy (adjective) *Obscene, lewd, indecent, smutty.*

In undermining religion through **bawdy** and slapstick humor, through circumspect allusions and emotive innuendos, Professor Kennedy is guilty of an injustice to and an imposition upon his students and the University.

beatific (adjective) *Exalting; radiant; suggesting a special blessedness.*

Her smile was **beatific,** and now she took the glass of sherry, but before she had finished it, her eyes closed. Maria took it from her hand, and Doña Leonarda slept.

becket (noun) *A simple device for holding something in place, as a small grommet or a loop of rope with a knot at one end to catch in an eye at the other.*

Racing to Bermuda in 1956, we would wear out a helmsman every half hour, even with the aid of a **becket** made out of several strands of shock cord.

beleaguered (adjective) *Hemmed in; bottled up: subjected to oppressive or grievous forces; harassed.*

What power did the Mayor of New York, or the **beleaguered** publishers, have to come to the aid of the public—in the wake of a generation's legislation granting special immunities to the labor unions who are free to conspire together in restraint of free trade?

belletrism (noun) *An interest in* belles lettres *to the neglect of more practical or informative literature; literary aestheticism.*

Though Chambers was a passionately literary man, always the intellectual, insatiably and relentlessly curious, in the last analysis it was action, not **belletrism,** that moved him most deeply.

belletristic (adjective) *Relating to the writing of* belles lettres; *speech or writing that consciously or unconsciously is more concerned with literary quality than with meaning.*

The special idealism of the youth who went to college or completed college during the postwar years seized on collective fancies. When these fell apart, they fell back to the paunch liberalism of the fifties, dressed up by the **belletristic** politics of Adlai Stevenson. The end came in Dallas.

bellicose (adjective) *Characterized by military hostility; provocatively warlike.*

The closeness of de Gaulle and Adenauer was a historical monument to the possibilities of trans-**bellicose** life.

bellwether (noun) *The guide by which one measures other data.*

The current airline industry load factor (i.e., the percentage of filled seats) is between 65 percent and 75 percent. And the **bellwether** price of a ticket (economy class, non-super saver) is greatly inflated.

beneficence (noun) *Active goodness or kindness.*

It is prudent to take reasonable precautions against the abuse of a beneficence; but it is not correct to evaluate a **beneficence** on its abuse-potential.

beneficently (adverb) *Kindly; charitably.*

Many years ago I asked the dean of my alma mater why no credit was given for the mastery of typing or shorthand and he replied **beneficently,** "There is no body of knowledge in typing."

Benthamite (noun) *After Jeremy Bentham, principal architect of utilitarian philosophy: one who adheres to the theory that the morality of any act is* *determined by its utility, and that pleasure and pain are the ultimate standards of right and wrong.*

The problem is to weigh the voting strength of all the categories and formulate a program that least dissatisfies the least crowded and least powerful categories: and the victory is supposed to go to the most successful **Benthamite** in the race.

bereft (adjective) *Deprived, especially by death; stripped; dispossessed.*

Miss Sayers contends that the faculty for logical thought is a skill of which the entire contemporary generation has been **bereft;** I note, but do not press the point.

bestir (verb) *To stir up; rouse into brisk, vigorous action.*

If the alumni wish secular and collectivist influences to prevail at Yale, that is their privilege. What is more, if that is what they want, they need **bestir** themselves very little.

bifurcate (verb) *To branch or separate into two parts.*

Yale shouldn't be turned over to the state because there are great historical presumptions that from time to time the interests of the state and those of civilization will **bifurcate,** and unless there is independence, the cause of civilization is neglected.

billingsgate (noun) *Foul, vulgar, abusive talk (named after a fish market in London where such talk was routine).*

The student was drunk, it was way past midnight, he had descended into the campus yard and there began a racist **billingsgate** at the expense of blacks, Jews, and Catholics.

blasé (adjective) *Apathetic to pleasure or life; indifferent as a result of excessive indulgence or enjoyment.*

I was asked whether I would consent to a public demonstration staged outside my office urging me to run. I was flabbergasted, but sought to act **blasé** about the whole thing.

blighted (adjective) *Withered or destroyed; disappointed or frustrated.*

The obdurate superstition, more widespread than anything since the number thirteen was **blighted** as unlucky, is that the rich are not paying their share of taxes.

boiserie (noun) *Carved wood paneling.*

The dinner was discreetly served in the Queen's Drawing Room, in the candlelight with the crystal **boiserie** effect and, always, the soft light, its Fauvist colors standing out in the mortuary of regal ancestors.

bombastic (adjective) *Pretentious, inflated.*

Anthony was incapable of pomposity. He cared more about effective relief for those who suffered than about **bombastic** relief for those who formed committees.

booboisie (noun) *The ignorant class. The term is H. L. Mencken's, and he self-evidently took pleasure in suggesting that the ignorant class was composed substantially of the bourgeoisie, normally thought of as the hard-working middle class.*

The critics of those who joined Senator Jesse Helms in protesting the use of public money to finance the "art" of Robert Mapplethorpe and Andres Serrano did a hell of a job of caterwauling about the provincialism of the **booboisie** who protested the exhibitions.

bowdlerized (verb) *Shrunk, with the purpose of expurgating titillating bits. After Thomas Bowdler (1754–1824).*

Churchill pauses from the war effort to cable back his regards to Mrs. Luce, who meanwhile has been asked by the Joint Chiefs of Staff to brief them on her analyses, which, suitably **bowdlerized,** appear in successive issues of *Life* magazine and are a journalistic sensation.

breviary (noun) *An ecclesiastical book containing the daily prayers or canonical prayers for the canonical hours.*

St. James's was dark except for candles on both sides of the sanctuary, the four dim lights overhead for tracing the aisles and the pews, the light inadequate for reading one's missal or **breviary.**

Brobdingnagian (adjective) *Huge. The word is from Jonathan Swift's imaginary country, inhabited by giants, in* Gulliver's Travels.

Finally Khomeini cried uncle, and, at age eighty-eight, set out to attempt to bring to Iran a small measure of the growing prosperity it was experiencing even while feeding the Peacock Throne the gold, frankincense and the myrrh it had taken to consuming with such **Brob-dingnagian** appetite.

bugaboo (noun) *A source of concern, especially something that causes fear or distress often out of proportion to its actual importance.*

As for the **bugaboo** that an element of internal debt is being passed on to future generations, it is "unmistakably false."

bugbear (noun) *An object of irritation or source of dread or abhorrence; especially a continuing source of annoyance.*

William Safire's **bugbear** is the statement made last week jointly by Secretary of State James Baker and Soviet Foreign Minister Alexander Bessmertnykh, "The ministers continue to believe that a cessation of hostilities would be possible if Iraq would make an unequivocal commitment to withdraw from Kuwait."

bull (noun) *An authoritative declaration or statement.*

Adult men and women, staring hard at a clause in the Constitution of the United States that forbids an establishment of religion and recognizing no reasonable nexus between that prohibition and the recital at their local public school of a public prayer jointly formulated by rabbis, ministers, and priests, receive on Monday what might be called a juridical **bull** from the Supreme Court, and on Tuesday there is compliance.

bumptiousness (noun) *The quality of one who is presumptuously, obtusely, and often noisily self-assertive.*

After it was all over, the student body president approached me with a wonderful combination of diffidence and **bumptiousness,** to say that he disapproved of the pig-bit, but that I was not to mistake this for approval of anything I had said, presumably not even the passage in my speech in which I deplored race prejudice.

buncombe (noun) *Talk that is empty, insincere, or merely for effect; humbug.*

Arafat's approach to a fresh plan in the Mideast was scorned by the government of Israel as so much diplomatic **buncombe.**

burden (noun) *The central theme; the principal idea.*

The front-page story (the *New York Times,* July 24) is headlined,

"H.U.D. Approved Rent Subsidies/ After Coors Wrote the Secretary." From the headline alone, the **burden** of the story is communicated.

burin (noun) *An engraver's tool having a tempered steel shaft ground obliquely to a sharp point at one end and inserted into a handle at the other.*

Not so much in the service itself, then, as in the recall of service, engraved and re-engraved gently but insistently by a dozen **burins,** decade after decade, will the idea of rendering service become lodged in the moral memory.

bursary (noun) *The arrangement by which students do work for the school or college in return for a remission of a part of their tuition or room and board.*

Sally worked at Vassar ten hours every week as a **bursary** student.

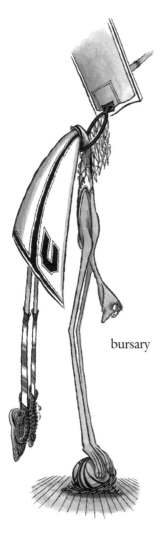

bursary

C

cacoëthes (noun) *An uncontrollable desire.*

I wink noisily at Rosalyn Tureck and suggest that who knows, the liqueur might just conceivably give her a case of **cacoëthes** piano-itis.

cadre (noun) *A nucleus or core group, especially of trained personnel or* *active members of an organization who are capable of assuming leadership or of training and indoctrinating others.*

Arafat, who looks like a gangster, often acted as one, and surrounded himself with a terrorist-minded **cadre** pleading the excuse that the Israelis deploy terrorists who need to be coped with.

caeteris paribus (adverbial phrase; Lat.) *If all other relevant things remain unaltered.*

Life for the average citizen, *caeteris paribus,* is about the same, except that in Venezuela any dissenting political activity was forbidden, whereas in Mexico only meaningful political activity is forbidden.

callow (adjective) *Lacking in adult sophistication, experience, perception, or judgment.*

Anthony Trust influenced Blackford from the time they were at school together in England just before the war, and Trust was in the fifth form and Blackford a **callow** third-former.

calumny (noun) *False charge or misrepresentation intended to blacken one's reputation; slander.*

The **calumny** Mr. Harriman attempted to pin on Mr. Rockefeller was that he would permit the Transit Authority to do the only thing the Transit Authority is permitted by law to do, namely, raise the fares.

canard (noun) *A false or unfounded report or story; a groundless rumor or belief.*

There exists an obdurate superstition that the rich are not paying their share of taxes. This **canard** is spread by the Congressional Budget Office, which is a propaganda arm of the Democratic Party that ought to be indicted by the Food and Drug Administration for feeding the general population dangerous stimulants.

candor (noun) *Directness of expression.*

It appears that Mayor Koch's most ingratiating quality, an unquenchable thirst for **candor,** was what finally did him in.

canon (noun) *A basic general principle or rule commonly accepted as true, valid, and fundamental.*

The **canon** of academic freedom is very clear: no one idea is to find corporate favor in educational institutions over another.

cant (adjective) *The expression or repetition of conventional, trite, or unconsidered ideas or sentiments.*

Boris old boy, although I am entirely committed to our cause, I find the repetition of the **cant** phrases of Communism altogether depressing.

capricious (adjective) *Given to changes of interest or attitude according to whims or passing fancies; not guided by steady judgment, intent, or purpose.*

What can be proved between competing crews on different boats? Not very much. There is a feature of ocean racing that can make a shambles of the whole thing. The poorest judgment can, under **capricious** circumstances, pay the handsomest rewards.

carapace (noun) *A protective covering similar to a hard bony or chitinous outer covering such as the fused dorsal plates of a turtle.*

They sat around a table in a soundproofed, bug-proof room situated within a **carapace** especially designed to frustrate any efforts at electronic intrusion.

caravanserai (noun) *An inn in Near or Far Eastern countries where caravans rest at night; usually a large bare building surrounding a court.*

Although Tito was prepared to spend cold nights in the trenches with his troops, he was manifestly happier in the **caravanserai** of the mighty.

cartelization (noun) *The organization of an industry or commodity in one or more countries so as to dominate commerce.*

The refusal of the principal European nations to defy their farm blocs has suggested the possible **cartelization** of the European economy in the next year or two.

Cartesian (adjective) *Relating to the philosopher Descartes, who specified direct and logical forms of thought and analysis.*

In an idle moment during a holiday, I searched the waveband of a portable radio in quest of something to listen to. None of the twenty or so options relayed classical music. It required only a little **Cartesian** *Geländesprung* to alight at the conclusion that it is the responsibility of the government to maintain monuments that are man-made, as well as those given us by nature.

Carthaginian (adjective) *Totalist, as in the Roman destruction of Carthage in 146 B.C.*

And one has therefore to pause before proceeding to hold every Iraqi responsible for the crimes of Saddam Hussein and those front-line sadists who disgraced the irreducible maxims of human decency. To consign them all to perpetual poverty is **Carthaginian** in moral architecture, and we must desist from doing this.

Carthusian (adjective) *Austerely self-disciplined, self-denying; relating to the Carthusians, members of an austere religious order founded by St. Bruno in 1084.*

Since anyone who chooses to do anything other than become a **Carthusian** monk is almost certain to pay taxes, the prospect of relief from ten thousand dollars in taxes is both real and appropriate.

catechetical (adjective) *Relying on questions and answers to inculcate orthodoxy.*

A sane man might seek to designate whatever figurative edifice shelters the household gods of American Liberalism, its high priests, its incense makers, and its **catechetical** press.

catechizing (verb) *Severe questioning designed to illuminate moral guilt.*

Tony Coelho, who has spent much of his adult life **catechizing** Republicans, fled office rather than submit to a public study of whether he has himself been submitting to the standards he has preached.

caterwauling (verb) *Complaining loudly; screeching.*

It is a story that has to do with all the **caterwauling** about nuclear waste and what to do with it.

Catonically (adverb) *In connection to Marcus Porcius Cato (149 B.C.), Roman statesman, or Marcus Porcius Cato (46 B.C.), Roman Stoic philosopher, both celebrated for austerity: repeated injunctions, or warnings, or predictions (e.g., "Delada Carthago est," Marcus Porcius Cato's "Carthage must be destroyed.").*

I haughtily, and indeed just a little sadly, remind Pat that Horrible Foo has, as, **Catonically,** I had always warned her he would, proved to be a wicked, wicked dog.

caudillo (noun) *A Latin American dictator, usually self-installed.*

The Americans still thought Castro a banana-republic **caudillo.**

cavil (noun) *A quibble; a frivolous objection.*

The **cavil** that Beethoven doesn't need looking after since his records sell by the trainload isn't at all satisfying to someone spelunking through radio channels in search of Beethoven.

cede (verb) *To give up, give over, grant, or concede, typically by treaty or negotiated pact.*

It is very dangerous to **cede** to a society the right to declare what are and what are not the freedoms worth exercising.

centripetal (adjective) *Moving, proceeding, or acting in a direction toward a center or axis.*

When stopped and everyone turns his eyes on me, I experience that mortification I always feel when I am the center of **centripetal** shafts of curiosity, resentment, perplexity.

centripetalization (noun) *The process by which things proceed in a direction toward a center axis.*

It was obvious to the conservatives who grouped together after the Second World War that the **centripetalization** of power simply had to be arrested.

chattel (noun) *Movable item of personal property, such as a piece of furniture, an automobile, a head of livestock.*

It was for this reason, said Mr. Thomas, that he could speak so eloquently on the subject of the Dred Scott decision, which reduced human beings—Negroes—to **chattels.**

chiding (noun) *Reproof, rebuke.*

Johnny turned to Blackford. "You and your goddam . . . continence." . . . [He] got orotund when he was tight, and Blackford smiled at the familiar **chiding.**

chiliastic (adjective) *Relating to the Second Coming; having to do with the reappearance of Christ on earth.*

That the existence of the Congress of People's Deputies, or of the Supreme Soviet, should have meaning at all is positively **chiliastic** in its implications.

chimera (noun) *An imagined idea, person, or fancy, unusually impractical, romantic.*

Turning his head abeam, the constellation his eyes fixed on had splashes of starry hair that shimmered, and eyes to steer by, and lips set in a pensive, seductive mode. He felt a luff in the sail, snapped his head forward to the mast, and quickly located his navigational star. He had wandered high on his course, while looking back at that **chimera** over Mexico.

chivalrous (adjective) *Marked by honor, fairness, generosity, and kindliness especially to foes, the weak and lowly, and the vanquished according to knightly tradition.*

Let us move towards a **chivalrous** candor, based on a respect for the essential equality of human beings, which recognizes reality, and speaks to reality.

circumlocution (noun) *Indirect or roundabout expression.*

She wanted to know what I was up to, and I told her about Vietnam, with the usual **circumlocutions.**

circumlocutory (adjective) *Marked by or exhibiting the use of an unnecessarily large number of words to express an idea; using indirect or roundabout expression.*

Smith was recalling to himself that he had taken great, **circumlocutory** pains never actually to deny his guilt directly to those who had most intimately befriended him.

clerisy (noun) *The well-educated or learned class; intelligentsia.*

The impact of the scientific developments that have absorbed the moral energies of our bishops and of the American **clerisy** in general prompts questions more basic than the question of selective conscientious objection.

climacteric (noun) *A decisive or critical period or stage in any course, career, or developmental process.*

The steel companies irked Murray Kempton by putting on a statistical passion play whose **climacteric** shows that if next summer the steel unions should go after and get higher wages, the American companies will no longer be able to compete with foreign steel companies.

cloying (adjective) *The special taste you get when something is repeated, or heard, or seen so often that it loses its original flavor and becomes simply boring.*

The lawyers are of course active, as also the anti–capital punishment organizations; but lawyers and generic opponents of capital punishment have a way of **cloying**—they sometimes leave the impression they'd have freed Jack the Ripper—and indeed they kept Ted Bundy alive for ten years.

coadjutor (noun) *A helper, assistant.*

"The Republican party," said Nelson Rockefeller—Lindsay's **coadjutor** in New York modern Republicanism—in the summer of 1963, "is the party of Lincoln."

coda (noun) *A concluding portion of a musical, literary, or dramatic work, usually a portion or scene that rounds off or integrates preceding themes or* *ideas; anything that serves to round out, conclude, or summarize yet has an interest of its own.*

Ah, the ideological **coda,** how it afflicts us all! And how paralyzingly sad that someone who can muse over the desirability of converting New York into an independent state should, having climbed to such a peak, schuss down the same old slope, when the mountains beckon him on to new, exhilarating runs.

codicil (noun) *A provision, as of a document, made subsequently to and appended to the original.*

"Do you mean, m-m-ma'am," the Prime Minister said to Queen Caroline, "those held in Great Britain by the United States, pursuant to the **codicils** of the NATO Treaty? Or d-d-do you mean those bombs over which we have total authority?"

cogency (noun) *The quality or state of appealing persuasively to the mind or reason.*

A young man cannot automatically be condemned for having acted frivolously if he sets out to weigh the demands of loyalty to this country's government against the **cogency** of the military objective he is being conscripted to risk his life for.

cognate (adjective) *Related to each other; analogous.*

Freedom of the press, freedom of speech—these **cognate** liberties are, of course, routinely construed to extend not only to journalism but also to expression of a more subtle kind, namely, artistic expression.

colloquy (noun) *A high-level, serious discussion.*

The Liberal Party's deliberations—which are a **colloquy** between Mr. David Dubinsky and Mr. Alex Rose—are copiously reported; and Adlai Stevenson, John Kennedy, and Lyndon Johnson all appeared in person to accept the Party's endorsement at great big to-dos.

colonic (adjective) *Having to do with the colon. [A high-colonic medical examination reaches up into the large intestine.]*

"I never went to Yale, Blacky, so I can't answer those high-**colonic** questions."

comity (noun) *Friendly civility, mutual consideration.*

The American President, the British Prime Minister and the Soviet despot make dispositions involving millions of people for the sake of temporary geopolitical **comity.**

commonweal (noun) *The common interest; the good-better society.*

The idea of a vote governed by an ethos of the **commonweal**—a voter's fiduciary obligation to vote not alone for his narrow best interest, but for the public interest—is substantially lost sight of as candidates gather together money from the lobbyists and settle down to lifetimes in the House of Representatives.

communization (noun) *The transformation of a person or movement into complicity with Communism, sometimes voluntary, sometimes forced.*

Dr. Alvaro Nueces had turned against Castro in 1960, protesting the **communization** of the 26th of July Movement.

complaisant (adjective) *Marked by an inclination to please or oblige or by courteous agreeability.*

Thornton Wilder had first to step over the body; he smiled at me as if he had negotiated a mud-puddle. The Master who followed Mr. Wilder smiled as well. His was less **complaisant.**

complementary (adjective) *Suggestive of completing or perfecting; mutually dependent: supplementing and being supplemented in return.*

Lindsay emphasized certain themes, foremost among them his own liberalism and his aloofness from the Republican Party. He developed a **complementary** theme, namely the necessity of saving New York City from the curse of reaction.

concatenation (noun) *A series or order of things depending on each other as if linked together.*

José López Portillo, the people's friend who left Mexico with a foreign debt of $90 billion, before he left office built, in addition to houses for himself and each of his children, an astronomical observatory, useful for tracing friendly astrological **concatenations,** if indeed Sr. Portillo acquired all the money with which he built his houses by speculation.

concert (verb) *To play or arrange by mutual agreement; to contrive or devise.*

I expect you will share your information with your superior. And if it becomes necessary, of course, the Prime Minister and the President will need to **concert** the postponements.

concupiscent (adjective) *Lustful.*

The Protestant theologian Dean Fitch reminds us that we have recently entered upon the most acutely degenerate of the stages of civilization: The Age of Love of Self. For a period we loved God; then we loved rationalism; then we loved humanity; then science; now we love ourselves, and in that **concupiscent** love all else has ceased to exist.

condign (adjective) *Deserved; appropriate; adequate.*

Abrams: A reporter, Paul Branzburg, was called to testify in front of a grand jury, and he took the position that he should not have to testify about material he had learned in confidence. The Supreme Court held five to four that he did have to testify. Mr. Branzburg subsequently left the state, and so far as I know has not returned to Kentucky.

WFB: Is that **condign** punishment?

conduce (verb) *To lead or tend, especially with reference to a desirable result.*

I sense intuitively that while friendship does not necessarily grow out of experience shared, experience shared **conduces** to a bond from which friendship can grow.

conflate (verb) *To bring together; collect, merge, fuse.*

Now, nobody is going to be able definitely to establish what happens for every million dollars a state spends on a national service program. Too many questions have to be **conflated** to permit a responsible prediction.

confutation (noun) *The act or process of overwhelming by argument.*

It is necessary in making one's complaints against the society we intend to replace, to be vague and even disjointed. To be specific, or to be orderly, is once again to run the risk of orderly **confutation**.

confute (verb) *To overwhelm by argument.*

Listening to Marshal Zhukov elaborate the virtues of Communism, President Eisenhower found himself "very hard put to it" to **confute** him.

congeries (noun) *A collection; accumulation; aggregation.*

I have seen only two political firestorms that resulted in sharp and immediate political response. The first was the sentencing of William Calley, the anti-hero of My Lai. The crowd simply insisted his penalty was inordinate, insisted on this for a **congeries** of reasons, primarily a frustration with the length and conduct of the Vietnam war.

consanguinity (noun) *The state of being related by blood or descended from a common ancestor; thus a close relationship or connection; affinity.*

John Lindsay might have waited until 1965 to oppose Jacob Javits in the primary, but such a move was out of the question by reason not only of political prudence but of ideological **consanguinity.**

construe (verb) *To put a certain meaning on something; to understand something in a particular way.*

Tamayo might be given an opening to **construe** a conversational jog in an unexpected way.

contemn (verb) *To view or treat with contempt as mean and despicable; reject with disdain.*

Samuelson would have us not only **contemn** the treatment of economics of such men as Jewkes, Hayek, Röpke, Anderson, Watt, and von Mises, we are also to doubt their motives.

contemporaneity (noun) *The quality or state of existing or occurring during the same time.*

They suffer, for one thing, from **contemporaneity.** What was allegedly done by the Democratic team is extremely current, whereas the Republicans came up with events some of which were three to eleven years old.

contiguous (adjective) *Immediately adjacent, in time or location.*

Lindsay Bradford was now engaged in conversation with a **contiguous** beer drinker.

continence (noun) *Self-restraint from yielding to impulse or desire.*

Johnny, opening the window to reach for another can of beer, discovered with horror that there were none left; and reaching into the cigarette box, discovered that he had simultaneously run out of cigarettes. He turned to Blackford. "You and your goddam . . . **continence.**"

contiguous

contraband (noun) *Goods or merchandise the importation, exportation, or sometimes possession of which is forbidden; also, smuggled goods.*

The trouble is, the Viets know that however much of the **contraband** they succeed in stopping at sea, the stuff is getting through.

contravene (verb) *To go or act contrary to; obstruct the operation of; infringe, disregard; oppose in argument; contradict, dispute.*

It does not take political courage to **contravene** one's own religion, it takes moral infidelity, of which I do not propose to be guilty inasmuch as I put the moral order above the political order.

controvert (verb) *To dispute or oppose by reasoning.*

I find it continuingly relevant, in a book on contemporary politics, to attempt to **controvert** controvertible misrepresentations.

contumacious (adjective) *Obstinately disobedient; rebellious; challenging the law.*
Francis Plimpton wrote to me, I replied, and toward the end of our correspondence he asked me to make publicly plain his own feeling about **contumacious** lawyers.

contumely (noun) *Disdain; expression of contempt, dislike, hatred.*
Has Michael Milken, in his revolutionary lifetime, re-situated the ethical norms of business conduct in such a way as to earn universal **contumely**?

convention (noun) *General agreement on or acceptance of certain practices or attitudes.*
Alice Goodyear Corbett (the **convention** had always been to use her full name, dating back to when, at age five, asked by a visiting Russian what her name was, she had answered, "*Moye imya* Alice Goodyear Corbett") had attended schools in Moscow from kindergarten.

cooptation (noun) *Election or selection, usually to a body or group by vote of its own members.*
The **cooptation** of the unions by the bureaucracy forwarded fascism of various kinds, including the militant and ideological fascism of Mussolini's Italy in which the state became precisely that object so correctly feared: the central unit of undifferentiated loyalty.

cordon sanitaire (noun; Fr.) *A line designed to act as a buffer between two territories actually or potentially hostile to each other.*
We arrive [at Fillmore East to hear Virgil Fox, the organist, play Bach], and there are hippies and non-hippies trying to get in, a sellout. One young man ventures forward, do I have an extra ticket? I give him one of the two tickets, thinking to keep the second, under the circumstances, as *cordon sanitaire.*

cornucopia (noun) *An inexhaustible supply, variety.*
"*Petit déjeuner, simple,*" she smiled at him, expressing admiration over the **cornucopia** he had ordered and was proceeding, with such wholesome pleasure, to devour.

cosmology (noun) *A view of the origin, structure, and (often) purposes of the universe.*

Jeff Greenfield wrote a withering piece for the *Yale Alumni Magazine* about an appearance I made at Yale which had begun with a press conference and went on to a formal speech. His piece was a stretch of arrant scorn for my thought, logic, diction, and **cosmology.**

cosmopolitanism (noun) *An excessive admiration and imitation of the cultural traits or achievement of others at the expense of the cultural identity or integrity of one's own land or region.*

Olga turned her head to one side and began to cry. She confessed that her parents had become afraid of having foreigners coming to their home, Comrade Stalin having pronounced recently on the dangers of **cosmopolitanism.**

coterie (noun) *A small group of people bound together by common interests or loyalties.*

Lieutenant Gallardo was in charge of the little **coterie** of bodyguards that surrounded Castro wherever he went.

coterminously (adverb) *Contained within the same period; coextensive.*

Allen Dulles was head of the CIA for nine years. During that period, and as a matter of fact since then, he and the CIA are criticized more or less **coterminously:** Allen Dulles was the CIA incarnate.

Couéism (noun) *A system of psychotherapy based on optimistic autosuggestion; the founder is best remembered for his adage "Every day, and in every way, I am becoming better and better."*

The wreckage of two world wars fought for democracy is made up of the collapsed surrealisms of the ideologues, who succeeded finally in pushing **Couéism** right over the cliff.

covenant (noun) *A rather solemn agreement, designed as binding.*

There is one aspect to the tax turmoil that asks for reflection. It is the unfortunate breach of the 1986 **covenant** at which time it was generally agreed that the tax committees of Congress would simply let things alone for a while and see how it all worked out.

Coventry (noun) *A state of ostracism or exclusion from the society of one's fellows.*

The irrepressible and irrational right-crackpot who advances an inanity—say that "Eisenhower and Kennedy have brought us to the brink of surrender"—is instantly identified as what he is, and the forces of opprobrium, social and intellectual, quickly maneuver to consign him to **Coventry.**

cozen (verb) *To deceive by artful wheedling or tricky dishonesty; to beguile craftily: victimize by chicanery; to act with artful deceit.*

It is easy to say that ideally you should stand still and be polite and attentive when addressed and **cozened** by the same man who that same morning berated you as a racist and hater.

credenda (noun) *The constituent elements of what forms your belief, in religion, politics, whatever.*

Imagine a reformist pope who questions the authenticity of the Bible, and you have some idea of the philosophical and spiritual problems that Gorbachev faces. He cannot deny the **credenda** of the Soviet state without denying at the same time his own legitimacy.

credo (noun) *A strongly held or frequently affirmed belief or conviction.*

The term "professionally competent," as used by the academic freedomites to describe a legitimate criterion of employment, can, under their **credo,** be meaningfully applied only to the "fact" aspect of teaching.

credulous (adjective) *Ready or inclined to believe, especially on slight or uncertain evidence.*

I have no quarrel with Mr. Seymour, although I should be perhaps less categorical—enough so, for example, to allow me to express preference for a **credulous** Democrat over a profoundly convinced Communist.

cryptic (adjective) *Having a hidden meaning, perhaps even impenetrable.*

Consuelo stood by the window of his office in downtown Mexico City after receiving the **cryptic** telegram from Miami. The assignment he had received from Rolando Cubela was startling.

cryptographer (noun) *One adept in the art or process of writing in or deciphering secret code.*

Blackford Oakes reappeared at James Street early in the afternoon, and said to Trust that he would like to consult with an Agency **cryptographer.**

cudgel (noun) *A short, heavy stick or club.* "*To take up the cudgels*" *is to enter into a vigorous contest.*

He says that he is not even sure whether, when his father dies, he will take up the **cudgels** of the House of Lords.

curio (noun) *Something arousing interest as being novel, rare, or bizarre.*

Why reissue the book? I think the reason for doing so is that it is a historical **curio,** and historical curios are often worth looking at, especially if they are unfamiliar to you.

cursory (adjective) *Rapidly, often superficially, performed with scant attention to detail.*

His introduction in that subject at Maxwell Field ("How to be useful if shot down and incorporated in the resistance movement") was **cursory.**

cynosure (noun) *A center of attraction or interest.*

Blackford's classmates were already dribbling into the classroom and, alerted to the cause of the excitement, looked instantly at the **cynosure** on the blackboard and exploded in squeals of delight and ribaldry.

D

danseur (noun) *The male dancer in a ballet group; often used to suggest said dancer's exhibitionistic impulses.*

George Bush was in Brussels deciding that he would, for once, take the arms control show away from the world's premier **danseur,** Mikhail Gorbachev.

declamation (noun) *A rhetorical speech; harangue.*

He is fiercely loyal to his family, while firm in insisting that he will not leave his fortune to the second generation as he doesn't believe in inherited wealth. That **declamation** drew a discreet wink from his devoted wife of forty-six years.

decoct (verb) *To figure out by deduction what the true meaning is of a statement, a symbol, an oblique communication.*

It isn't easy to **decoct** the machinists' message from the picket signs or from public pronouncements.

decorous (adjective) *Marked by propriety and good taste, especially in conduct, manners, or appearance.*

And how long are the professors willing to wait before a **decorous** opportunity presents itself for exposing the steady drive in the direction of collectivism that has gathered so much momentum at Yale over the past dozen years?

decrepitude (noun) *A state of ruin, dilapidation, or disrepair; lack of power; decay.*

If indeed the nation is united behind Mr. Eisenhower in this invitation to Mr. Khrushchev, then the nation is united behind an act of diplomatic sentimentality which can only confirm Khrushchev in the contempt he feels for the dissipated morale of a nation far gone, as the theorists of Marxism have all along contended, in **decrepitude.**

defi (noun) *A challenge; rejection of.*

Tom Wolfe had published *The Painted Word*, a **defi** hurled in the face of the art critics, challenging their taste, questioning their originality, and lamenting their power.

deify (verb) *To glorify or exalt as of supreme worth or excellence.*

The Department of Economics is not alone in **deifying** collectivism.

demagogue (noun) *Someone who appeals for public support by saying, or promising, that which most appeals to the crowd, or mob, he is addressing.*

Noriega is an effective **demagogue.** And—always a winner in Latin America—he has defied the United States of America and got away with it.

démarche (noun; Fr.) *A course of action; maneuver; a diplomatic representation or protest.*

He could not now report that his diplomatic initiative had worked in such a way as to give the Soviet Union the opportunity to use its great resources to stall the German *démarche* planned by the Western powers.

demurral (noun) *The act of taking exception.*

He permitted himself a smile as he shot out his trigger finger to the door, which was the director's way of saying, "Out"—to which there was no known **demurral.**

denature (verb) *To change the nature of; take natural qualities away from.*

What the Pope does say with such heartening fidelity is that socialism is an extravagant historical failure and—more—that socialism has a way of **denaturing** human beings by giving power to a central government which tends to use that power to suppress the individual and to come up with false gods for him to worship, like nationalized railroads (the example is mine, not His Holiness's).

denominate (verb) *To give a name to; call by a name; designate.*

The Cold War is a part of the human condition for so long as you have two social phenomena which we can pretty safely **denominate** as constants.

dénouement (noun; Fr.) *The final outcome, result, or unraveling of the main dramatic complication in a play.*

Blackford gave Joe the plot, but not the *dénouement,* and as they were driving home Joe expressed himself as genuinely indignant at Iago, and Blackford told him that was a really good sign.

deprecate (verb) *To disapprove of, often with mildness.*

It is a part of the Japanese tradition to exhibit great modesty, to disparage one's accomplishments, to **deprecate,** even, one's most sacred opinions.

depreciate (verb) *To make to seem less valuable or important; to diminish in value.*

Sir Alistair said to Queen Caroline, "Ma'am, I cannot believe that you **depreciate** natural curiosity, even if you don't exhibit it."

deracinate (verb) *To separate from one's environment.*

Randall Jarrell was saying Serious Things. He was describing a morally and intellectually **deracinated** environment in which students are encouraged to cut their ties to the world of standards and norms.

deracination (noun) *Cutting off cultural and institutional and ethnic ties, leaving the individual, or tribe, or nation without its traditional support system.*

A European figure so august that ladies curtsy when they are presented to him was telling the table at which we all sat about the great mischief being done by the missionaries in Venezuela who move in on native tribes and totally break down their cultural order, resulting in **deracination** and chaos.

derogate (verb) *To make to seem lesser in esteem; disparage, decry.*

Salesmanship is nowadays **derogated,** the assumption being that a salesman is somebody who persuades you to do something you do not want to do.

derogation (noun) *Disparagement; belittling.*

[*WFB posing a question to Allen Dulles*] What is your opinion of the continued **derogation** of the intelligence function? Why should the CIA be made a—a sort of general laughing stock?

desiccate (verb) *To drain of vitality, especially to divest of vigor, spirit, passion, or a capability of evoking mental or emotional excitement.*

I have suggested that the principal difficulties of the beginning ocean sailor are (1) the mystifying lack of expertise in much of what goes into ocean sailing; and (2) the tendency in some experts to **desiccate** the entire experience by stripping it of spontaneity, or wonder.

desideratum (noun) *That which is desired; the better, or even perfect, state.*

Jesse Jackson began by saying that for a black, his blackness is forever the supreme fact of life. In saying so, without suggesting that he lamented this priority, he moved very far from Martin Luther King's Dream, in which color made no difference: color-blindness isn't a **desideratum** for Jackson.

desultorily (adverb) *Lacking steadiness, fixity, regularity, or continuity.*

However **desultorily,** his father always kept in touch with him, and the more easily as his son grew older, and the two, though apart, did not grow apart.

determinism (noun) *The doctrine that all acts of the will result from causes which determine them in such a manner that man has no alternative modes of action.*

One needs to remind oneself that under Marxism–Leninism it is the people who are supposed to be the vehicle of historical **determinism.** It fits nowhere in Soviet doctrine for the people to assert themselves in favor of reforms which the Kremlin opposes.

detritus (noun) *Products of disintegration or wearing away; fragments or fragmentary materials.*

The experience would touch the young, temperamentally impatient with any thought of the other end of the life cycle, with the reality of old age; with the human side of the **detritus** whose ecological counterparts have almost exclusively occupied fashionable attention in recent years.

de trop (adjective) *Too much or too many; in the way; superfluous; unwanted.*

The swanks at PBS are pretty proud of their audiences, but an exchange in Latin would probably be thought **de trop.**

detumesce (verb) *To subside from a state of swelling; to diminish in size.*

Brother Leo in his monastic cell consulted the diary he kept of his activities, and counted nine visits to the Alargo mansion to see Josefina Delafuente. He went to the chapel, and on his knees prayed most earnestly. He tried to distract himself, but the daemon would not **detumesce.**

detumescence (noun) *The collapse of what was heretofore stiff.*

Surely it was with malice aforethought that he permitted the ash on his burning cigarette to grow to advanced **detumescence.**

deviationist (adjective) *Departing from the principles of an organization (as a political party) with which one is affiliated.*

One can say, "disciples of Communism, en bloc, follow the Moscow line." That is a responsible generalization, unaffected by the fact of schismatic flare-ups or **deviationist** sallies.

devolution (noun) *Passing down from stage to stage; the passing of property, rights, authority, etc., from one person to another.*

It is jarring to recall that as recently as during this century, Wales and even Scotland were discussing the kind of "**devolution**" that would have meant, in effect, self-rule.

devolve (verb) *To cause to pass down, descend, be transferred, or changed; to* *transfer from one person to another: hand down; to pass by transmission or succession.*

John Lindsay was to stress repeatedly the nonpartisan nature of his own candidacy, assiduously cultivating the air of transcendence that **devolves** to a candidate too big for any single party.

dialectic (noun) *Any systematic reasoning, exposition, or argument that juxtaposes opposed or contradictory ideas and usually seeks to resolve their conflict; play of ideas; cunning or hairsplitting disputation.*

During those months, a fascinating **dialectic** went on. Herbert Matthews would write that American prestige was sinking in Cuba—on account of the aid the U.S. Government was giving to Batista. Our Ambassador in Havana meanwhile complained to the State Department of the demoralization of the Batista government—on account of our failure to provide aid.

diapasonal (adjective) *A musical term which suggests fully orchestrated; full; harmonious.*

The documents they were given to read were in many respects lurid, melodramatic—preposterous even, so their exchanges were not always in the **diapasonal** mode when one of the young CIA agents would interrupt his reading to make a comment or ask a question.

diaphanous (adjective) *Of such fine texture as to be transparent or translucent.*

Three hours later they were in the suite Hilda shared with Minerva: two bedrooms, the living room between them dimly lit by lamps covered in only barely **diaphanous** pink.

didactic (adjective) *Characteristic of the teacher, whether in manner, or arrangement, or posture.*

"I am glad to hear your Spanish is so good, Blacky. And I, Professor Sally Partridge, am competent to test how good it is." She appeared briefly in the doorway in her dressing gown, affecting her **didactic** posture at the lectern.

dilate (verb) *To write, or speak about, at great or greater, length.*

[*WFB speaking to Mortimer Adler*] You begin by reaching a very interesting conclusion which I would like to hear you **dilate** on, namely that it doesn't really matter whether there was a prime mover [i.e., a force that created the first earthly thing].

dilettante (noun) *A person who cultivates an art or branch of knowledge as a pastime without pursuing it professionally.*

Professor Kirkland does not believe that academic freedom ought to protect the pedant, the **dilettante,** or the exhibitionist.

diminution (noun) *Diminishing; lessening; decrease.*

Ask then, would we be better off chucking the opposition to federalized medicine? If we did this, there would be, assuming the validity of the findings above, an instant **diminution** in costs.

discountenance (verb) *To put to shame; reject; abash, disconcert; refuse to look upon with favor.*

It is an interesting conjecture that the effect of the Republicans' closed shop is not only to **discountenance** a useful bloc of Republican voters but to discourage a potential flow of voters whose background is Democratic, and who might well view the Conservative Party as a way-station to a remodeled Republican Party.

discursive (adjective) *Wandering from one topic to another; rambling; desultory; digressive.*

[He is] a very old friend about whom I wrote in a **discursive** book that I think of him as the most wholesome young man I have ever known.

disestablishmentarian (noun) *An advocate of disestablishing or altering the existent state or national institution.*

The English Establishment rests on deeply embedded institutional commitments against which the Socialists, the angry young men, the **disestablishmentarians,** have railed and howled and wept altogether in vain.

disfranchisement (noun) *The deprivation of a statutory or constitutional right, especially of the right to vote.*

To deprive him of his vote it becomes necessary to deprive others like him of their vote, hence what amounts to the virtual **disfranchisement** of the race in Southern communities that fear rule by a Negro majority.

disingenuous (adjective) *Lacking in candor; not straightforward; crafty.*

Congressional retaliation is based on attempting to fix in the public mind that the President anticipated revenues of ABC, a growth rate of XYZ, and interest rates of GHI—and that these were defective as predictions and **disingenuous** in conception.

disinterested (adjective) *Taking a position—political, moral, analytical—which has no bearing on the position that would suit your own personal interests, because your interests are simply not involved.*

They seek to dramatize a point that choicers should force themselves to acknowledge is entirely **disinterested,** even as demonstrators for civil rights were fighting not for themselves, but for others.

disjunction (noun) *The action of disjoining or condition of being disjoined; separation, disconnection, disunion.*

He [Jesse Jackson] is given to the most grating verbal rhetorical **disjunctions** in contemporary language. ("We're going from the outhouse to the White House." "They've got dope in their veins rather than hope in their brains.")

dislocation (noun) *A disruption of the established order.*

My host lightly probed me. I told him the truth, that I had heard the not so sotto voce impoliteness on the part of the student. He apologized for the social **dislocation,** and explained that the young man's father was a legislator who reversed himself and cast a deciding vote to relax the abortion law, in punishment for which he had failed at reelection, and that son was overwrought, particularly against conservative Catholics.

dislocative (adjective) *Causing confusion; causing to deviate from a normal or predicted course, situation, or relationship.*

Many people shrink from arguments over facts because facts are tedious, because they require a formal familiarity with the subject under discussion, and because they can be ideologically **dislocative.**

dispossess (verb) *To remove from someone the possession especially of property or land; put out of occupancy; eject, oust.*

What we deplore is what Saddam Hussein went on to do. Where is the Democrat who was urging all along that we consummate Desert Storm by marching into Baghdad and **dispossessing** Saddam?

disquietude (noun) *Lack of peace or tranquillity.*

A man formally aligned on the other side of the political fence endorsing all your major platforms has the effect of relieving you of the **disquietude** that the existence of alternative approaches to government necessarily poses.

disquisition (noun) *A formal or systematic inquiry into or discussion of a subject; an elaborate analytical or explanatory essay or discussion.*

Bui Tin began one of his rambling, historical **disquisitions** on the history and culture of the region.

dissimulation (noun) *Deception; hiding under a false appearance.*

Then there is someone who oscillates from sarcasm to **dissimulation.** You would think he had tipped his hand conclusively by beginning his letter, "Dear Mr. Pukeley."

dissipation (noun) *Wasteful expenditures and intemperate living.*

What he is, is an undisciplined Catherine's wheel, whose columns read like angry and disordered reflections of the previous night's **dissipations.**

dissolute (noun) *A person lacking in moral restraint.*

One of the two technicians added that Heath seemed very bored with the work at hand, that he tended to arrive late for work in the morning, and that he had acquired a reputation for being something of a **dissolute,** patronizing the local bars, often with a girl.

dissonant (adjective) *Marked by a lack of agreement; incongruous, dissident, discrepant.*

Why has the same nation that implicitly endorsed the social boycott of Soviet leaders changed its mind so abruptly—to harmonize with so **dissonant** a change in position by our lackadaisical President?

dithyrambic (adjective) *Truly exaggerated in praising something or somebody.*

In recent weeks we found ourselves interrupted in our **dithyrambic** praise for democracy when the guy in El Salvador whom we did not like won.

dittify (verb) *To turn into a ditty—a song or short poem, especially one of simple, unaffected character.*

"Remember: *Qui cogitat quod debet facere, solet conficere quod debet facere.*" Mr. Simon beamed as he attempted to **dittify** his maxim in English: "Those who think about their duty/Are those who end by doing their duty!"

doctrinaire (adjective) *Stubbornly devoted to some particular doctrine or theory without regard to practical considerations.*

Mr. Lindblom dislikes a **doctrinaire** attitude toward anything. He incessantly encourages the pragmatic approach to economics. It naturally follows that any reliance on absolutes, or any reference to indefeasible "rights" is unwarranted and anachronistic.

dour (adjective) *Marked by sternness or severity.*

Georgianna opened the door, black and **dour** as ever, but instantly docile when Blackford said, "Georgy, lend me a dollar quickly."

dowdy (adjective) *Not modern in style; staid, shabby.*

She would never have got that **dowdy** kind of life with me, but that's what she wanted.

doxology (noun) *Praise to the Deity; thanksgiving for divine protection rendered anaphorically, i.e., repetitious in formulation. E.g., "Blessed be God/ Blessed be His holy name/Blessed be His son Jesus."*

I would not expect in a serious conversation with a Cardinal about great affairs that he would punctuate his message with bits and pieces of Christian **doxology.**

doyen (noun) *The senior male member of a body or group; one specifically or tacitly allowed to speak for the body or group.*

So well known is Herbert Matthews as **doyen** of utopian activists that when in June of 1959 a Nicaraguan rebel launched a revolt, he wired the news of it direct to Mr. Matthews at the *New York Times*—much as, a few years ago, a debutante-on-the-make might have wired to Walter Winchell the news of her engagement.

dramaturgical (adjective) *Pertaining to the art of writing plays or producing them.*

It is somewhere recorded that, reciting a speech written for him by one of his entourage, which speech he had not even read over before delivering it, [Huey Long] reached a line in which he thought the trace of a tear theatrically appropriate, engineered that tear without any difficulty, and later on casually commented on his proficiency in these **dramaturgical** matters.

dreadnought (noun) *A heavily armed battleship; hence, something or someone that cannot be stopped.*

With my Kaypro 386, plus Path-Minder, plus Desq View, plus SideKick, plus Daniel Shurman of Humanware to make sense of it all, I am something of a **dreadnought** on a word processor.

dudgeon (noun) *A sullen, angry, or indignant humor.*

The Most Reverend Ernest Trevor Huddleston arrived at the makeshift studio at the nave of St. James's Church in Piccadilly in full Episcopal regalia, and in very high **dudgeon.**

dulcet (adjective) *Done in quiet, sweet, soft tones.*

The question arises of the fear of a united Germany, a fear widely expressed, if mostly in **dulcet** tones, by Europeans east and west of Berlin.

duplicity (noun) *Deception by pretending to entertain one set of feelings and acting under the influence of another.*

I have charged Yale with **duplicity** in her treatment of her alumni.

dysgenically (adverb) *Genetic profusion of a kind thought inimical to public interests.*

Israel does not like the fact that most Russian Jews express a wish to settle down not in Israel but in the United States because it needs a Jewish population to guard against being **dysgenically** overwhelmed by Arabs who procreate with the speed of light.

dyspeptic (adjective) *Bitter; morose; spastic.*

George Gilder was working for the *New Leader* magazine, having graduated from Harvard a few years earlier. In **dyspeptic** protest against the Republican Party's nomination of Barry Goldwater, he and a friend had written a book called *The Party That Lost Its Head*—i.e., the GOP, by nominating Goldwater.

dysphasia (noun) *Loss of or deficiency in the power to use or understand language caused by injury to or disease of the brain.*

> *Reporter:* But Mr. Lindsay said today that he never knew you at Yale at all—
>
> *WFB:* Well, I'm surprised he said that because it's not true. If he is suffering from some sort of **dysphasia**, that would make a whole lot of his recent behavior understandable.

E

eclectic (adjective) *Varied; reflecting different styles, doctrines, methods.*

> Knowing Mr. Kennedy's appetite for **eclectic** reading matter, he gave him J. H. Plumb's *Sir Robert Walpole* and a volume of Betjeman's poems.

ecumenical (adjective) *Having the backing of more than one faction, political, theological, or scientific.*

> Two ideas are current, neither of them the property of conservatives or of liberals. It is an **ecumenical** mix, with some conservatives arguing that the show is up for world Communism, some liberals arguing that it is much too early to tell.

edify (verb) *To instruct and improve, especially in moral and religious knowledge; enlighten, elevate, uplift.*

> Transform the Peace Corps into a body of evangelists for freedom, young men and women highly trained in the ways of Communist psychological warfare who could in behalf of freedom, analyze, argue, explain, and **edify**.

efface (verb) *To eliminate clear evidence of; to remove from cognizance, consideration, or memory.*

> On those occasions when the Republican Party of New York has won municipal elections it has done so precisely by **effacing** any distinguishable characteristics of the Republican Party.

effete (adjective) *Soft or decadent as a result of overrefinement of living conditions or laxity of mental or moral discipline.*

> Etiquette is the first value only of the society that has no values, the **effete** society. An occasional disregard for the niceties may bring us face to face with certain facts from which man labors to shield himself.

efficacious (adjective) *Bringing about an intended result.*

I find it continuingly relevant, in a book on contemporary politics, to attempt to controvert controvertible misrepresentations because it is especially interesting to inquire whether they tend to be **efficacious** or not.

effrontery (noun) *Act of shameless audacity and unblushing insolence.*

What they ought to be condemning is what I once called the special **effronteries** of the twentieth century. One of these—eastern seaboard liberalism—substituted ideology for metaphysics, causing the great void which the sensitive of whatever age feel so keenly.

effulgence (noun) *Strong, radiant light; glorious splendor.*

Kenneth Tynan is not a reasoner and his story about appearing before the Senate Internal Security Subcommittee goes on with its poetic **effulgence.**

effusion (noun) *Unrestrained expression of feelings; something that is poured out with little or no restraint, used especially of self-expression.*

Kenneth Tynan is a young man of letters well enough known among the literati in England because of his precocious **effusions** against the established order.

egalitarian (noun) *Equalist; one who believes in the doctrine of equalizing the political and economic condition of everyone.*

The novelistic urge of the great ideological **egalitarians** who write books with such titles as *The Ugly American* has been to invest in their protagonist in the CIA appropriately disfiguring personal characteristics.

egalitarianism (noun) *A belief that all men are equal in intrinsic worth and are entitled to equal access to the rights and privileges of their society; specifically, a social philosophy advocating the leveling of social, political, and economic inequalities.*

The adjacent fraternities are far gone in desuetude, for reasons nobody entirely understands, though everybody agrees they have something to do with the affluence-cum-**egalitarianism** paradox.

egregious (adjective) *Flagrant; distinctively presumptuous, horrible.*

Recent amendments to the Constitution have merely codified popular passions. But (save for the largely irrelevant exception) there has been no constitutional amendment the purpose of which was to revise the interpretations of a Supreme Court, notwithstanding **egregious** provocations by the Court, most recently during the '50s and '60s when it became commonplace to refer to the "Warren Revolution."

élan (noun; Fr.) *Enthusiastic vigor and liveliness.*

The aide pondered the communication, its rather special *élan,* and made the decision to put the whole dossier into the Director's In box.

eleemosynary (adjective) *Of or relating to charity.*

I intended to probe the question whether an inverted kind of subsidy, to middle and big business, was going on under our **eleemosynary** noses— by encouraging, with social welfare schemes, a cheap labor market.

elegy (noun) *A poem or song of lament for the dead.*

Milton wrote an **elegy** to a young man dead, and Bach wrote music searingly beautiful, his own tribute to a departed brother. One must suppose that Milton wept over his poetry, and Bach over his music.

elide (verb) *To suppress or alter at intermediate stages.*

When a politician has got so given to thinking of himself as a collectivity that he is capable of writing in his diary, "At 8 A.M., we got up and took a shower," he has **elided** from modesty to something else.

elixir (noun) *A concoction held to be capable of prolonging life indefinitely; something that acts potently upon one, invigorating or filling with exuberant energy or cheer.*

The first course was an omelet of sour cream and tomatoes, an *elixir* unlike anything Black had ever tasted, and better.

emanation (noun) *A flowing forth; a quality or property issuing from a source.*

Although Harriet Pilpel was as sharp in debate as any Oxford Union killer, she managed a benevolent **emanation** that, I like to think, after twenty years of carpet-bombing exchanges with her, genuinely reflected her character.

emendation (noun) *The word or the matter substituted for incorrect or unsuitable matter.*

The new conservatives, many of whom go by the name of Modern Republicans, have not been very helpful. Their sin consists in permitting

so many accretions, modifications, **emendations,** maculations, and qualifications that the original thing quite recedes from view.

empirical (adjective) *Originating in or based on observation.*

The **empirical** spirit is interesting both because it is organically American ("if it works, it's good"; "nothing succeeds like success") and because
pride is a hugely important factor in the operation of governments,
which after all are run by human beings.

emplace (verb) *To put into position.*

The Israelis **emplaced** their nuclear-capable Jericho-2 missiles in hard-
ened silos and in September 1988 mounted their first satellite launch.

encysted (adjective) *Enclosed in a cyst, capsule, or sac.*

Do we need to describe how bad the scene is in Detroit? It is the **encysted** home of unemployment and unrest, on account of unemployment plus the racial tensions that are engendered in communities in
which whites and blacks vie for desperately needed jobs.

endemic (adjective) *Widespread; taking hold throughout a community or
society.*

A great, indeed a massive, change was under way in America in the late
fifties, the beginning of an **endemic** disenchantment with American
liberalism.

engender (verb) *To bring into existence; give rise to.*

They spent a relaxed hour talking about this and that, with that odd
sense of total relaxation **engendered** by the knowledge of great tension
directly ahead.

enjambement (noun) *Continuation in prosody of the sense in a phrase beyond the end of a verse or couplet; the running over of a sentence from one
line into another so that closely related words fall in different lines.*

" 'Against welfare,' says a woman supporter in a tall magenta hat, 'and
not making New York a haven for . . . well . . .' She says no more." So
writes *The New Yorker.* Now, great big grown-up people can effect the
enjambement without strain. The lady in the magenta hat was anti-
Black!

enjoin (verb) *To direct, prescribe, or impose by order, typically authoritatively and compellingly.*

Assuming that the Yale graduate, a potential entrepreneur, is an inveterate, dauntless gambler and decides to run all these risks and launch his business, there are further considerations that his economists have **enjoined** him to keep in mind.

ennobling (adjective) *Tending to elevate in degree or excellence.*

Whatever byways, on the road to this final Third Act, George Bush may have missed, this is the time to adjourn any complaints about them and to concentrate on an **ennobling** performance.

enumerate (verb) *To relate one after another.*

The Declaration of Independence goes on to **enumerate** the grievances of the colonies. It is a stirring catalogue, but it finally reduces to the matter of the source of power, i.e., who should rule?

envoi (noun) *The final communication; valedictory; send-off.*

The portrait of Ronald and Nancy Reagan done by Mike Wallace for *60 Minutes* was their **envoi** to the republic on their presidency.

ephemera (noun) *Things of transitory existence, interest, or importance.*

The whole thing [Mike Wallace's farewell interview with President and Mrs. Reagan on *60 Minutes*] seems a cheerful mix of nostalgia and **ephemera,** but the portrait was genuine and will be studied (or should be) by future biographers.

epicene (adjective) *Sexless; lacking in vigor, virility.*

To spend one hour with a principal British political figure without any critical attention being given to the leaders of the Labour Party or to his critics within the Conservative Party would make for an **epicene** hour.

epicurean (adjective) *Suited to a person with refined taste, especially in food and wine.*

Blackford laughed. "This dinner is **epicurean** by comparison with what you poor English boys have to eat at your fashionable schools, and how do I know that? You guessed it, I was indentured in one."

epigoni (noun) *Close followers, given to imitating, or being bound by, the star they become the creatures of.*

William Winpisinger, the president of the striking (Eastern Airlines) machinists, is a socialist and is quick to put a class struggle aspect on any labor-management division, and indeed Mr. Winpisinger lost no chance to do this. And the **epigoni** jumped in. Sure enough, there was Jesse Jackson joining the picketers.

epiphany (noun) *The illuminating meaning of an experience; the sudden penetration of a heretofore elusive truth.*

As he tapped out his message, the **epiphany** crystallized. His redemptive mission was incandescently clear. He, Rolando Cubela, would kill Fidel Castro.

epistemological (adjective) *Pertaining to the philosophical discipline that has to do with learning; how we learn.*

Is it correct or incorrect to view the adversary process as an **epistemological** process? Will it lead us to the truth, or is it more likely to be described as something which leads us to the only bearable means by which we will agree to proceed in deciding whether to put this guy in jail or not?

epistemology (noun) *The study of the method and grounds of knowledge, especially with reference to its limits and validity.*

In an age of relativism one tends to look for flexible devices for measuring this morning's truth. Such a device is democracy; and indeed, democracy becomes **epistemology:** democracy will render reliable political truths just as surely as the marketplace sets negotiable economic values.

epochal (adjective) *Extremely important, likely to affect future events or the understanding of them.*

During the tumultuous month since being told he would be returning to Cuba on an important mission, he had been given intensive training. And then had come the **epochal** briefing the day before his departure, delivered by Malinovsky himself.

eponym (noun) *A person whose name gave meaning to a word that became common.*

Billy Budd is practically an **eponym** for—innocence; purity.

equanimity (noun) *Evenness of mental disposition; emotional balance, especially under stress.*

Those of us who do not go year after year wondering whether tomorrow will bring yet another war threatening our survival will perhaps find it difficult to understand the relative **equanimity** of the Israeli people.

equerry (noun) *One of the officers of the British royal household in the department of the master of the horse in regular attendance on the sovereign or another member of the royal family.*

An **equerry,** introducing himself genially, supervised turning the car over to a chauffeur, and Blackford's luggage to a footman.

eremitical (adjective) *Characteristic of the hermit; far removed from ordinary life and considerations.*

To say that Mrs. Jones is unbiased in the matter of Colonel North because she was unaware of him, notwithstanding that Colonel North dominated the news in the press, on radio, and on television for about three weeks two springs ago, isn't to come up with a fine mind that missed the entire episode because she was absorbed in **eremitical** pursuits.

eristic (adjective) *Finely argumentative; taking logic and argument to extreme lengths.*

Any failure by beneficiaries of the free world to recognize what it is that we have here, over against what it is that they (the Communist world) would impose on us, amounts to a moral and intellectual nihilism: far more incriminating of our culture than any transgression against **eristic** scruples of the kind that preoccupy so many of our moralists.

errantry (noun) *A roving in quest of knightly adventure.*

The liberals' mania is their ideology. Deal lightly with any precept of knight-**errantry,** and you might find, as so many innocent Spaniards did, the Terror of La Mancha hurtling toward you.

eructation (noun) *A violent belching out or emitting.*

He knew that the center of their earth was heaving and fuming and causing great **eructations** of human misery in its writhing frustration over the failure of Soviet scientists to develop the hydrogen bomb at the same rate as the Americans.

erudite (adjective) *Possessing an extensive, often profound or recondite knowledge.*

"If you are not aware of it," said the Queen, "I am sure there are several members of this **erudite** company who will explain it to you."

eschatological (adjective) *Pertaining to the ultimate ends of life, existence.*

It became clear—years ago, for the perceptive; only recently, for the true believers—that Communism does not work, i.e., Communism does not bring on the redemptive **eschatological** paradise predicted by Marx, does not ease the burden of the worker, and does not reduce the power of the state.

eschatologically (adverb) *In a manner dealing with the ultimate destiny of mankind and the world.*

The Communists' program is capable (at least for a period of time, until

eschatologically

the illusion wears off) of being wholly satisfactory, emotionally and intellectually, to large numbers of people. The reason for this is that Communist dogma is **eschatologically** conceived.

eschew (verb) *To turn down; ignore; disdain; do without.*

The United States has two sovereign responsibilities at this point. The first is to maintain our guard. The second is to **eschew** any invitations to finance the economic rehabilitation of the Soviet Union.

esoterica (noun) *Items intended for or understood by only a few.*

Fleetwood had been designated to give the first toast. After that, he turned his **esoterica** into a single metaphor that suggested the pre-eminent concern all civilized persons must have for peace.

espousal (noun) *A taking up or adopting as a cause or belief.*

Despite protestations that Professor Davis had failed to qualify for promotion, it was plain for all to see that he had been eased out because of his outspoken criticism of capitalism, his **espousal** of numerous left-wing causes, and his attacks on several large financial trusts and holding companies with which various members of the Yale Corporation were affiliated.

essay (verb) *To make an attempt at.*

> The operator evidently knew only a single word of English, which sounded like, "Outzide, outzide." He **essayed** first French and then German, to no better end, and then the cinders of his Russian.

establishmentarian (adjective) *Allied to the dominant institutional forces.*

> The most hotly contested primary of the postwar season was that of New Hampshire, when in 1964 the grass roots forces of challenger Barry Goldwater did a pitched battle with the **establishmentarian** forces of Nelson Rockefeller.

estop (verb) *To put an end to; bar; prohibit.*

> Is it suggested that a defense secretary who had been to a cocktail party, or even one who had gone to bed drunk, would **estop** the flow of instructions from the President?

ethnocentrism (noun) *The belief that one's own ethnic group, nation, or culture is superior to all others.*

> I had in mind journalism and the academy, though perhaps most conspicuous at the time I wrote (1965) was the entrenched **ethnocentrism** of certain unions, in which a job is something you deed to your son or son-in-law, if he is faithful.

eudaemonia (noun) *Happiness derived through a lifetime devoted to fulfilling moral obligations.*

> Her doubts are of course shared by many who are discouraged by the failure of general education to achieve **eudaemonia.**

euphonious (adjective) *Pleasing in sound.*

> The forces of fascism were not quite ready to give up, but that would come. Meanwhile, if he had to serve as a lord—Lord Fleetwood? Rather **euphonious**—why, he would simply have to do so.

Eurocentric (adjective) *Regarding Europe as the central historical, intellectual, and cultural concern for American students.*

> Ten lashes is about what some of us had in mind as appropriate for those in Stanford who succeeded in abolishing the theretofore compulsory

courses in Western culture, deemed too "**Eurocentric.**" It has yielded to a required course called Cultures, Ideas, and Values.

evanesce (verb) *Gradually to disappear.*

Marx and Engels promulgated the view that if you eliminate private property, all derivative vices **evanesce.**

evanescent (adjective) *Tending to vanish or pass away like vapor.*

I and the "Panic" have a way of provoking the unreasoned and impulsive resentment of sailors whose view of ocean racing tends to be a little different from my own. That resentment is wholly spontaneous and, I like to feel, **evanescent.**

eventuate (verb) *To come out finally or in conclusion; come to pass.*

His fluent French and schoolboy knowledge of English and Japanese suggested a clerical career, which never **eventuated** because a few months after his seventeenth birthday the Japanese surrendered.

evocation (noun) *The act or fact of calling forth, out, or up; summoning, citation.*

Mr. Lindsay first discovered that the idea of taking positive action to relieve New York City of the curse of drug addiction can best be summed up in the haunting **evocation** of "concentration camps."

ex cathedra (adverb; Lat.) *Authoritatively; by virtue of or in the exercise of one's office, as with papal authority.*

The public is being trained, as regards the Supreme Court of the United States when it is interpreting the Constitution, to accept its ruling as if rendered *ex cathedra,* on questions of faith and morals.

excogitation (noun) *Something thought up and said or written or pronounced. There is an implication of derision, or contempt, when the word is used.*

Roe v. *Wade* was a lousy decision, perhaps even an indefensible act of constitutional *excogitation,* and the choicers know that they are safest by not asking the Court to look again at this century's version of the Dred Scott decision.

excretion (noun) *The process of eliminating useless, superfluous, or harmful matter.*

The conservative rejection of the John Birch Society, of the anarchists and other fanatics, was an act of **excretion** essential to political and intellectual hygiene.

execrable (adjective) *Deserving to be declared evil or detestable.*

Crew A, out of an egregious ignorance and showing **execrable** judgment, elects to go around Block Island north to south.

execration (noun) *The act of cursing or denouncing.*

The Iranians, after they have done with the rituals of **execration,** are going to want that which is universally popular. Cars, rock music, Bloomingdale's.

exegete (noun) *A person skilled in critical explanation or analysis, especially of a text.*

WFB: You say that the rights of lawyers and priests should extend to journalists.

Abrams: As a general matter, yes. There are some differences, but as a general matter, yes, I—

WFB: That's sort of a revolutionary accretion and yet, in asserting that point, you tend to do so as an **exegete** of the Constitution rather than as a somebody who wants to amend it.

exegetical (adjective) *Pertaining to critical explanation or analysis.*

"I understand Bolshevik theory and do not need your **exegetical** help in this matter."

exhibitionistic (adjective) *Behaving so as to attract attention to oneself; extravagant or willfully conspicuous.*

In the Gulf, notwithstanding the **exhibitionistic** can-can by Gorbachev during the final hours, it was never conceivable that a nuclear power would stand in the way of our military strategy.

exigency (noun) *The hard requirements of a situation.*

We must bear in mind that the scholar has not one but two functions. These pursuits are (1) scholarship, and (2) teaching. They are related solely by convenience, by tradition, and by economic **exigency.**

exiguous (adjective) *Scant; meager.*

Five years later, the general prosperity of commercial television edged *Firing Line* over toward public broadcasting (commercial television could not afford to give up the revenue a program like *Firing Line*, with its **exiguous** ratings, displaced).

ex officio (adverb; Lat.) *By virtue of an office.*

About a year ago, Senator Nunn suddenly announced that the stricter of two plausible versions of the ABM ban on testing was the correct one, and I swear it was like the pope pronouncing **ex officio** on a question of dogma.

exogamous (adjective) *Of or relating to or characterized by marriage outside a specific group, especially as required by custom or law.*

I am allergic to **exogamous** comparative dollar figures, so widely used in workaday polemical chitchat, such as, "For the cost of landing a man on the moon, we might have built one million one hundred thirty-seven thousand and eight low-middle class dwelling units."

exorcise (verb) *To get rid of the evil content of something.*

President Seymour had made a clarion call for a return to Christian values in 1937, but that did not **exorcise** the extreme secularism that characterized Yale at least during the last four years of his administration.

expedient (noun) *Something that is suitable, practical, and efficient in achieving a particular end; fit, proper, or advantageous under the circumstances.*

I herewith request Mr. Charles Buckley to do me, and the voters of New York, the favor of ending the confusion by the simple **expedient** of changing his name.

expertise (noun) *An operative body of knowledge.*

For those on the radical Left and for so many on the moderate Left, the true meaning of our time is the loss of an operative set of values—what one might call an **expertise** in living.

expiate (verb) *To make up for; atone for.*

During those ninety days he came to terms with himself. He decided that he could not **expiate** the sin he had committed against an innocent man until he had undertaken a great and heroic task of redemption.

expostulate (verb) *To plead earnestly in an effort to persuade or correct.*

That afternoon, Nicolai Pushkin shouted himself hoarse and spent himself to the point of exhaustion. His thickly built guard did nothing while Pushkin **expostulated,** except to read, seated at his desk, his comic book.

expostulation (noun) *Strong demand; remonstrance.*

With no further attention paid to his **expostulations,** his arms were strapped to his sides with the stretcher's harness and he was lifted into the ambulance and deposited alongside the cab driver.

expunge (verb) *To obliterate completely; annihilate.*

"You, Comandante Fidel Castro," Kirov said, "are my sovereign. You, by your example in Cuba, will illuminate the Marxist movement throughout the world, and perhaps even **expunge** the cruel and barbaric Marxism being practiced in the Homeland of Lenin."

extirpate (verb) *To wrench out; destroy; exterminate; remove any traces of.*

In his late crazy days, as distinguished from his early crazy days, Mao Tse-tung decided that Mozart and Beethoven were great public enemies of the revolution and sought to **extirpate** them and others from the inventory of music the Chinese were permitted to listen to.

extortionate (adjective) *Characterized by, or having the nature of, extortion; excessive; exorbitant.*

This requires negotiating with the Saudis to peg the oil price at a reasonable level for, say, twenty years. Without the cooperation of the Saudis, OPEC can never reassemble its **extortionate** cartel.

extravasate (verb) *To force out or cause to escape from a proper vessel or channel.*

Can the revolutionary essence be **extravasated** and be made to diffuse harmlessly in the network of capillaries that rushes forward to accommodate its explosive force?

extrinsic (adjective) *Unrelated to the person or matter or idea at hand; extraneous.*

Maria later realized that she reached maturity only that day, at that moment: she felt a concern entirely **extrinsic** to her own interests.

extrude (verb) *To disgorge; push out; thrust out.*

She looked up at a young, bearded man who, **extruding** the envelope from her hand, said to her politely but firmly, *"Seguridad, Señorita."*

extuberance (noun) *Protuberance.*

Seville—At a little kiosk near the park is a child's mechanical rocking horse. You insert 25 pesetas, and for ten minutes your little boy or girl rocks around the clock, gasping with pleasure while holding on hard to the little wood **extuberances** that serve as bridles.

exult (verb) *To be extremely joyful, often with an outward display of triumph or exuberant self-satisfaction.*

Most recently the Dartmouth administration's mills ran overtime to **exult** over the appearance, alongside the weekly's logo, of an anti-Semitic remark taken from Hitler's *Mein Kampf.*

eyrie (noun) *A room or a dwelling placed high up.*

Blackford was struck by the ornamental splendor of the scene, with the huge chandeliers, the gilt-red balcony, the steps behind him ascending to the regal **eyrie** whence Queen Caroline had descended.

F

factionalism (noun) *The process of splitting into parties, combinations, or cliques.*

Boris Andreyvich Bolgin could hardly help hearing—experiencing—vibrations of—a mounting division. There was **factionalism,** spying on one another, the sense that no leader without the strength of Stalin was truly a leader.

fallacious (adjective) *Embodying or presenting a false or erroneous idea.*

The administration of Yale, and the president in particular, dwell from time to time on the merits of laissez-faire education, hinting that there exist some alumni with contrary notions—notions which are, of course, demonstrably **fallacious.**

fallow (adjective) *Marked by inactivity.*

It had been more than an entire college generation since he had mingled with the hard left community, either students or faculty. Even the Russian he had learned, he was encouraged to let lie **fallow.**

fasces (noun) *A bundle of rods having among them an ax with the blade projecting, borne before Roman magistrates as a badge of authority in ancient Rome; the authority symbolized by the fasces.*

Jimmy Jones had his **fasces,** and from all accounts they were liberally used to keep in line those whose restive intelligence or natural hedonism questioned the ideals or resisted the spartan regimen.

fastidious (adjective) *Fussy about details; meticulous.*

Among other assets, Maria Raja had a second passport. Her mother, a refugee from Hitler's Hungary, was above all things **fastidious** about security arrangements.

fatuous (adjective) *Silly; thoughtless; inane.*

So much for Tom Wicker's **fatuous** attempt to make his frantic point that the fate of Owen Lattimore is now being visited on Tom Foley by the ass in the Republican National Committee who wrote a silly memo from which only silly people would conclude that the charge was made that Tom Foley is gay.

Fauvist (adjective) *Markedly vivid.*

A single early Picasso was lit by a shaft of soft light, its **Fauvist** colors standing out in the mortuary of regal ancestors.

fealty (noun) *The fidelity of a vassal or feudal tenant to his lord; faithfulness, allegiance.*

Congressman Lindsay voted with the Democrats a total of thirty-one times. As such, he was runner-up among liberal Republicans in the frequency of his **fealty** to Democrats-in-a-jam.

fecundity (noun) *Fruitfulness; fertility.*

The story quotes me directly: "We do have similarities to the Kennedys," says Bill. "Our wealth, our **fecundity,** our Catholicism. Other than that, the comparison is engaging but misleading."

ferula (noun) *A cane, or rod, used as an instrument of punishment; usually a flat piece of wood, sometimes encased in leather.*

Since it is pre-decided that the Bush Administration will not advocate the legalization of drugs, the Bennett basket is going to have to be chock-full of **ferula** with which to beat offenders.

fervent (adjective) *Having or showing great emotion or warmth; ardent.*

He greatly missed those **fervent** evenings with the select few, the brainy idealists who recognized that the Soviet revolution was the twentieth century's way of saying no to more world wars, to imperialism, to the class system.

fetid (adjective) *Smelly, rotten.*

The Republican candidate for President should devote himself absolutely to making the atomization of the Marxist myth an official crusade, one to which we will attach ourselves as vigorously as if we were spreading the word of how to extirpate smallpox from the **fetid** corners of the world.

fiduciary (adjective) *Of, having to do with, or involving a confidence or trust; of the nature of a trust.*

In its administration of the funds, the government does not meet orthodox **fiduciary** standards of the kind stipulated by the laws of most of the states for private insurance companies.

filigreed (adjective) *Adorned with a pattern or design resembling ornamental work of fine wire of gold, silver, or copper.*

"My dear Mr. Oakes," he read in a **filigreed** but authoritative hand that tilted sharply to the right. "I leave you to your researches during the morning and early afternoon."

fillip (noun) *Something added that tends to arouse or excite; a stimulating or rousing agent.*

When Lord Keynes brushed aside the demurrals of a critic concerned with the long-run effect of his program by saying "In the long run we are all dead," he originated a verbal **fillip** that made its way quickly into the annals of definitive retort.

fissiparous (adjective) *Reproducing by fission.*

The tribulations of the **fissiparous** Soviet empire will almost certainly guarantee, at least for the short run, a huge number of refugees.

flaunt (verb) *To exhibit with the view to attracting attention.*

Successful men are not necessarily ascetic men, and although a public is within its rights in declining to elevate to the presidency a candidate who **flaunts** his immorality, it is simply mistaken to suppose that failed marriages and occasional draughts of good spirits ruin the night of our kindly and gentle nation any more than they ruined the wedding at Cana.

fleeted (adjective) *Feliciitious; starry; piquant.*

Blackford wondered whether his path and the Queen's would even cross. He half hoped they would not; half hoped they would, three years having passed since their fleeting, **fleeted** encounter.

flippant (adjective) *Treating or tending to treat with unsuitable levity that which is serious or to which respect is owing.*

References to genitalia are as effective in the classroom as they are at a bachelor party, and **flippant** allusions to sacrosanct subjects are as delightful from the podium as from the soapboxes of Hyde Park.

flotsam and jetsam (nouns) *These terms usually appear together to refer to that part of the wreckage of a ship and its cargo found floating on the water or washed ashore. The phrase "flotsam and jetsam" now has an extended meaning of "useless trifles," "odds and ends."*

The **flotsam and jetsam** of Edward Bennett Williams's arguments wash up on the shores of reason in irreconcilable pieces, but on he goes, unperturbed.

flout (verb) *To treat with contempt; defile; mock.*

The problem with attempting eloquence at the United Nations is that that which is affirmed by all the surrounding moral maxims is regularly and systematically **flouted.**

fons et origo (nouns; Lat.) *The source. Literally, the fountain and origin.*

Mikhail Gorbachev can criticize Constantin Chernenko and Leonid Brezhnev—and Brezhnev can criticize Nikita Khrushchev, who criticized Stalin; but no one will criticize the *fons et origo* of all that poison, Lenin.

foppish (adjective) *Pertaining to or characteristic of a man who is preoccupied with and often vain about his clothes and manners.*

Mr. Mussolini was in his mid-forties, tall and angular. He was well dressed; the Director thought him even rather **foppish.**

forensic (adjective) *Pertaining to rhetoric used to plead a point.*

There has been some dissatisfaction over the President's speech. Hardly surprising. It was a magnificent **forensic** performance.

forswear (verb) *To renounce earnestly, determinedly, or with protestations.*

In other words, the South African government was slipping some money (a relatively modest one hundred thousand dollars, one is told) to that domestic force which **forswore** violence, Communism, and boycotts— over against its opposition. What it did was illegal. But hardly evil.

fractious (adjective) *Tending to cause trouble as by disobedience to an established order; hard to manage or unmanageable; refractory; unruly.*

Teenagers caught and convicted of felonies will be either put in jail or released in the recognizance of their parents. Said parents would have the right to surrender authority over **fractious** children by invoking probationary sentences.

fulmination (noun) *Vehement menace or censure; something that is thundered forth.*

Rubirosa has come to town. **Fulminations,** of course, are in order, but how pleasant **fulminations** can be at the hands of a master.

fulminator (noun) *One who denounces, sends forth censures or invectives.*

The 1,267 members of the freshman class of Yale University have been warned against the Moral Majority by President A. Bartlett Giamatti. And what a speech it was: Jerry Falwell, head of the Moral Majority, is said to be quite a **fulminator** himself.

fulsomeness (noun) *Copiousness, abundance so great as to become offensive.*

John Kennedy so oversold some of his own apostles on the general subject of his being the best qualified to serve as President of the United States that some of them went on to commit sins of **fulsomeness** which, one hopes, deeply embarrassed him.

fungible (adjective) *Returnable or negotiable in kind or by substitution; interchangeable.*

Although the age of computers and satellites and television dishes has done much to circulate ideas hitherto pockmarked in totalitarian cavities, in fact knowledge isn't all that **fungible.**

furtive (adjective) *Stealthy; surreptitious; hidden.*

Fidel Castro had got out of the habit of **furtive** midnight meetings, far removed from the handy personal and political apparatus he had got so used to which, with the push of a button, would get him a world leader on the telephone.

fusilier (noun) *Rifleman; soldier armed with a fusil (musket).*

Deng Xiaoping is seized, in Karl Wittfogel's phrase, with the megalomania of the aging despot, and rather than acknowledge the right of his citizens peaceably to assemble in order to petition the government for a redress of grievances, he shoots them; and, tomorrow, may hang those his **fusiliers** missed.

fustian (adjective) *Overblown; pompous; wordy.*

The only thing we can reasonably do isn't, at this point, **fustian** retaliation.

G

gainsay (verb) *To deny; ignore; overlook.*

It was not true that the liberal element within the Republican Party was willing to hand the party over to the right. There was no **gainsaying** the political influence of such prominent Republican liberals as Senator Charles Mathias.

gambol (verb) *To bound or spring about as in dancing or play; skip about; frisk, cavort.*

"Not tomorrow," said Caroline. "Wouldn't do for me to **gambol** about the woods on my horse while they are lowering Queen Benedicta into the sod."

Gemütlichkeit (noun; Ger.) *Coziness; good nature, kindliness, cordiality.*

The loneliness of flight is not entirely overwhelmed by cabin movies, the drinks, the food, the *Gemütlichkeit* of shoulder-to-shoulder life.

ASSEMBLY MEMBERS ONLY

MAP ROOM

gerrymander

gerrymander (noun) *An electoral district carved up without regard to demographic symmetry, intending to fortify a particular political party at the expense of another political party. The word is also used as a (transitive) verb.*

The fat and rich Democratic **gerrymanders** are going to find a dragon waiting for them when they rev up for the decennial hanky-panky. Those interested in self-government should side with the dragon, Newt Gingrich.

gibbet (noun) *An upright post with a projecting arm for hanging the bodies of executed criminals in chains or irons; gallows.*

Now everybody knows you shouldn't talk about **gibbets** to executioners, especially not when they happen also to be head of state.

gird (verb) *To prepare for a struggle, test of strength, or other action.*

I cannot complain softly. My blood gets hot, my brow wet, I become unbearably and unconscionably sarcastic and bellicose; I am **girded** for a total showdown.

Goo-gooism (noun) *From the initials of "good government," a reform movement in politics, especially in the era of Theodore Roosevelt—usually used disparagingly.*

If John Lindsay won, Republicans in Ohio and California would not be permitted to pass off his victory as meaningless, as merely a triumph of **Goo-gooism** in a jaded municipal situation.

grandiloquence (noun) *Lofty, extravagantly colorful, pompous, or bombastic style, manner, or language.*

Ramsey Clark is now and then just a little grandiose, e.g., "Dissent has been the principal catalyst in the alchemy of truth," which, substituting as it does "in the alchemy of" for the simpler "of," suffers not only from straitened **grandiloquence,** but from an edgy syntactical ineptitude.

granitic (adjective) *Very hard; granite-like.*

Now if you think this is because there is **granitic** resistance within Vassar to students of non-white background, how do we account for it that the presidents-elect of the senior class and the student government are black, and the junior class president-elect is Asian-American, and the president-elect of the sophomore class is Hispanic?

gravamen (noun) *The central point of a complaint; the heart of an accusation or objection.*

The **gravamen** of James Baldwin's complaint was that the *Times*'s publication had aborted the publication by *Playboy* magazine of Baldwin's speech, imposing a financial sacrifice on him of the $10,000 he had been told *Playboy* would pay him.

gravitas (noun; Lat.) *The kind of solemnity one associates with kings, bishops, and wise men; used in Rome to designate the mien of thoughtful, civic-minded, wise men.*

The key figure, of course, is Senator Nunn, around whose judgments *gravitas* closes in like clouds gathering around a prophet.

gravometer (noun) *A geological instrument designed to detect deposits of oil.*

This morning Murray Kempton speaks of the emergence of Romney as a presidential contender. Like a **gravometer,** he is attracted to the irony of the situation.

gregarious (adjective) *Seeking and enjoying the company of others.*

Clare Boothe Luce became ill. She was alternately reclusive and **gregarious** in the six months that were left.

grotesquerie (noun) *Something suggestive or resembling grotesque decorative art or the figures or designs of such art; something grotesque.*

There originated in this Couéism the reckless stampede to inflate the electoral lists, culminating in the **grotesquerie** of the state of Georgia, which voted in 1943 to give the vote to every eighteen-year-old.

guilelessly (adverb) *Innocently; naïvely; in an unsophisticated manner.*

Professor Kennedy subverted the faith of numbers of students who, **guilelessly,** entered his course hoping to learn sociology and left with the impression that faith in God and the scientific approach to human problems are mutually exclusive.

gull (verb) *To make a dupe of; cheat, deceive.*

Dr. J. B. Matthews painstakingly listed the names of dozens upon dozens of the unfortunate clergymen who had collaborated with the Communist movement, and finally reckoned that, percentagewise, more ministers had been **gulled** into supporting Communist fronts than teachers and lawyers.

H

habituate (verb) *To make familiar through use or experience; to make acceptable or desirable.*

They had walked almost eight miles that day, the fifth day of Blackford's exploration, and he was **habituated** now to the redundancy of the Trail's surrounding features.

hagiographer (noun) *A writer of biography of an idealizing or idolizing character.*

"For John Lindsay, the device of playing up 'the candidate' rather than 'the party' has been startlingly successful." But as if to guard against the perils of an untoward de-Republicanization, the **hagiographer** cautiously adds: "He identified himself with Senator Javits, former Mayor La Guardia and others."

hagiography (noun) *The writing or study of lives of the saints.*

But Lenin, himself as close as any man could be to heartlessness, understood intellectually the need for icons. And as a political matter, he'd have approved the **hagiography** of Communism, not because he believed in

LEXICON

the elevation of ideological saints, but because he'd have found it useful to accelerate the revolution.

hauteur (noun) *An assumption of superiority; an arrogant or condescending manner.*

Very soon after, we were back in Connecticut, and I strained to speak like Mortimer Snerd, so as to disguise from my friends the ignominy of my foreign experiences. The fashion is to comment on the **hauteur** of my diction.

hebdomadal (adjective) *Meeting or appearing once a week; weekly.*

Sometime after Adlai Stevenson announced his candidacy for President in 1952, he telephoned his former wife and told her to prepare the "boys" to be picked up on Sunday. Sure enough, photographers were there to record the **hebdomadal** piety of Adlai Stevenson.

hector (verb) *To fuss over insistently, intending to press a point.*

Blackford had made a passing effort to detoxify Sally during senior year at Yale, but hadn't since **hectored** her (or anybody else) on the subject of smoking.

hedonism (noun) *An ethical doctrine taught by the ancient Epicureans and Cyrenaics and by the modern utilitarians that asserts that pleasure or happiness is the sole or chief good in life.*

Less conspicuous problems must be thought of as having an economic impact: the instability of family life, listlessness at school, a growing national tendency to corruption, or **hedonism;** and insensitivity to suffering; a callousness that breeds ugliness of behavior.

hegemonic (adjective) *Pertaining to preponderant influence and authority, to the point of excluding other influence.*

In order to maintain the pressure that orients the Soviet Union and China toward reform in the first instance, we need to continue to roam those quarters of the world where the Soviet Union continues to exercise **hegemonic** influence.

hegemony (noun) *Preponderant influence or authority; leadership; dominance.*

Since Moscow is still willing to pay $14 million per day to continue to support Fidel Castro, Daniel Ortega reasonably hopes to hang on to that incremental Soviet subvention necessary to eliminate any possibility that the tatterdemalion Contras will ever seriously challenge the Marxist **hegemony** in Nicaragua.

hegira (noun) *A journey or trip, especially when undertaken as a means of escaping from an undesirable or dangerous environment or as a means of arriving at a highly desirable destination.*

All of New York was wired to trip him up—local police, FBI, California sheriffs. In the interval, Edgar Smith undertook a **hegira.** He went deep into Pennsylvania, in search of a cemetery, he said later, at which he could meditate.

hemidemisemiquaver (noun) *A sixty-fourth note; i.e., thoughts or frustrations lasting for only passing seconds.*

hemidemisemiquaver

As, wearily, he slid into bed at three in the morning for the second successive night, he blanked out what his musical colleague at Trinity liked to call the "**hemidemisemiquavers.**"

hermetically (adverb) *So as to be impervious to outside interference or influence.*

His brown eyes were either sound asleep (that was when Rufus was given over to analysis, parting company with his surroundings as though **hermetically** insulated from them) or fiercely active.

heterodoxy (noun) *An unorthodox opinion or doctrine.*

The president of the Conservative Book Club assigned *Message from Moscow* to readers, who reported back against it, on the grounds that the author's own prejudices were in favor of socialism; and such **heterodoxy** a small minority of CBC readers would not tolerate even as they would not have tolerated the distribution of *Animal Farm* in the light of Orwell's persistent inclination toward socialism.

heuristic (adjective) *Providing aid or direction in the solution of a problem but otherwise unjustified or incapable of justification; heightening curiosity about further scholarly or scientific exploration.*

Conservatives know that some human beings, as Albert Jay Nock stressed in his **heuristic** lectures at the University of Virginia, are educable, others only trainable.

hew (verb) *To cling; to adhere; to hold tightly to.*

As often as not Anthony would take the opportunity to **hew** to the lewd, low road.

hierarchical (adjective) *Of or relating to a classification of people according to artistic, social, economic, or other criteria.*

I note a kind of **hierarchical** polarization going on. When I was at college, it would have been unprecedented to refer to the President of the University other than as "Mr. Seymour." Today, the president is "President Schmidt." Back then, a professor was—"Mr. Whitehead," which is also what he'd have been called by his students. Today he would be "Dr. Whitehead," and his students would call him Chuck.

hirsute (adjective) *Hairy; covered with hair.*

Fidel was of course **hirsute,** while Rolando had only the trace of a shadow. He wondered whether to shave, as he would do if he were going to a social engagement, or to leave his chin as it was.

histrionic (adjective) *Theatrical; stagey.*

Usually the two men were alone when Tamayo reported his commission had been completed. When that was so, they would both break out into raucous laughter after their **histrionic** exchange.

holographic (adjective) *Written in the hand of the person from whom it proceeds.*

A dotted line from the lips of the master led to a balloon, within which Blackford, imitating the **holographic** style of his teacher, who a few days earlier had explained the English evolution ("micturate") of Caesar's word to describe his soldiers' careless habits when emptying their bladders, indited the words: "Mingo, Mingere, Minxi, Mictum."

homiletic (adjective) *Of the nature of a sermon; having the intention of edifying morally.*

Reagan: Do you mean, bad as Congress has been all this time with praying, they want us to take it now without praying?

WFB: I think that what you said is so **homiletic** it might itself be unconstitutional.

homily (noun) *A lecture or discussion on a moral theme.*

Senator Moynihan and Anthony Lewis charge that Ambassador Jeane Kirkpatrick and her legal adviser, Allan Gerson, are ignorant of the law. Moynihan added the **homily** that even though the Soviet Union does not abide by the law, that doesn't mean we shouldn't.

homophobe (noun) *One who dislikes, disapproves of, or has an irrational hatred of homosexuals or homosexuality.*

If a student these days opposes some of the demands of the Gay Liberation types, he might be branded as a **homophobe,** when all that can verifiably be said about him is that he is opposed to homosexual practices, which is still, though perhaps only just still, a permissible position.

honorific (noun) *Titles or other forms designed to suggest titles or honors earned or received.*

There were those who believed that no one in memory would ever outshine the brilliant young Luís Miguel, dressed now like an Italian movie star, with a tiny palette of colors below his handkerchief pocket, the flora and fauna of Latin American **honorifics.**

hortatory (adjective) *Using language intended to incite or to mobilize.*

The police reached the man, who had moments before jumped onto the stage and danced there naked, but poor Ken Galbraith, although he plowed a straight furrow through his **hortatory** address to the effect that the earth would open up and swallow us all if Nixon was reelected, was not able to engage the distracted audience.

hubris (noun) *Overweening pride or self-confidence; arrogance.*

The only autonomy liberalism appears to encourage is moral and intellectual autonomy; solipsism. And that is the autonomy of deracination; the philosophy that has peopled the earth with atomized and presumptuous social careerists diseased with **hubris.**

humbuggery (noun) *An attitude or spirit of pretense and deception or self-deception.*

There were those who are free of the superstition of liberalism who joined in denouncing Pérez Jiménez's "election"; for his offense was one of **humbuggery.**

hurly-burly (noun) *Confusion, turmoil, tumult, uproar.*

I never got around to it, in part because of the lack of time, in part because, of course, it would not, in the **hurly-burly,** have been publicly pondered.

husbandry (noun) *The careful, non-spendthrift management of your money.*
Faith Partridge's **husbandry** did not make her lose all perspective.

hydra-headed (adjective) *Having many centers or branches (from the Hydra, a mythical many-headed serpent).*

The imperative that worldwide attention be given to stop the traffic in **hydra-headed** arms beckons as never before.

hypermammiferous (adjective) *Having extremely large breasts.*

The late Congressman Adam Clayton Powell, Jr., once took a highly publicized trip to Greece with a **hypermammiferous** blonde. He was investigating Greek affairs. Congressman Powell, contemplating the bust of Homer.

I

icon (noun) *Object or person attracting worshipful attention.*

Sally was slightly withdrawn, indomitably independent in spirit, dazzling to look at if you began by discarding as irrelevant most of the competition in **icons** of the day—she didn't look like Rita Hayworth or Marilyn Monroe.

ideologize (verb) *To absorb within a system, so as to make it a part of that system.*

Che Guevara's concern with medicine was by now almost totally **ideologized.** He cared less how to cure someone suffering from a burst appendix than that the treatment should be the responsibility of the state.

idiomatic (adjective) *Verbally informal.*

"The principal liquid asset is the ten thousand dollars paid by the government when your brother was killed. Faith—your mother—managed to get your father's signature on that check"—Cam Beckett was a family friend as well as attorney, and Sally did not resent his **idiomatic** references to the family situation.

ignominious (adjective) *Marked by, full of, or characterized by disgrace or shame; dishonorable; deserving of shame.*

Mr. Leonard Hall added his voice to the chorus of breast-beaters after the **ignominious** defeat of Senator Goldwater.

ignominy (noun) *Deep, personal disgrace.*

I am perfectly at home in a small boat, and would, in a small boat race, more often than not come in if not on the side of glory, perhaps this side of **ignominy.**

ignoratio elenchi (noun; Lat.) *A fallacy in logic of supposing that the point at issue is proved or disproved by an argument which proves or disproves something not at issue.*

Lindsay ignored the challenge a half-dozen times, and finally replied to it by saying: "I don't know why you ask me to renounce Adam Clayton Powell, Jr., since Powell has come out for Mr. Beame." A classic example of what the logicians call ***ignoratio elenchi.***

impalpable (adjective) *Incapable of being felt by the touch.*

Boris knew to take the nearest church exit, keeping his eyes down, under no circumstances looking about him, lest his eyes fall on the intangible, **impalpable** Robinson.

impenitent (adjective) *Not repenting of sin; not contrite.*

Norman Mailer and a dozen others signed an advertisement in papers throughout the country under the sponsorship of a group called the Fair Play for Cuba Committee. The episode was less farce than an act of tragedy, though without dire consequence for the players—they are strikingly **impenitent** and insouciant.

imperturbability (noun) *The quality or state of being extremely calm, impassive, assured, and steady.*

I have seen consternation on the faces of more experienced members of my crew at such evidences of inexperience or even ignorance, and I do not myself pretend to **imperturbability** when they occur.

imperturbable (adjective) *Resolutely calm; unshakable; collected.*

The official Castro of tonight, Che reflected, bore little resemblance to the **imperturbable** private Castro of Sierra Maestra.

impetuosity (noun) *Undisciplined thought or action.*

He has the faculty, where legal problems are concerned, of releasing, say every fifteen minutes or so, a gossamer blanket over your **impetuosities.**

implacable (adjective) *Incapable of appeasement or mitigation; inexorable.*

Castro kept both radio sets on, but after a while turned them down. There was the faint monotonic sound of people talking, from the one set and, from the other, the muted beat of the rock music, **implacable** in its cacophony.

importune (verb) *To press or urge with frequent or unreasonable requests or troublesome persistence.*

He wondered whether he would ever again feel so close a kinship as he had felt for the two men he had just now got killed. With morbid shame he recalled **importuning** them to request a transfer, after V-E Day, so that they could serve out the balance of their terms with him.

imposture (noun) *A fake; a substitute of an unreal for the real; an act of deception.*

At the U.N., you regularly hear the totalitarians proclaim that genuine freedom is social and economic security. For that reason, there is "freedom" in East Germany, but not in West Germany. The argument is philosophically an **imposture**—just to begin with—because "freedom" is properly defined as an absence of constraint from man-made impediments.

imputation (noun) *The act of laying the responsibility or blame for something falsely or unjustly.*

Blackford knew all about Meachey. He had led the Oxford Committee to protest the **imputation** of guilt to Stalin during the show trials in the late thirties.

impute (verb) *To attribute accusingly, often unjustly.*

I assume that a Communist is a pro-Communist, though Tom Wicker sometimes acts as though it would be an act of McCarthyism to **impute** pro-Communism to Joseph Stalin, let alone Mikhail Gorbachev.

incertitude (noun) *Absence of assurance or confidence.*

Either the Supreme Court will more or less laze up to different specific cases in different ways, leaving the question of what are and what aren't the rights of parties in dispute, in boundless **incertitude,** or else basic laws will have to be rewritten.

inchoate (adjective) *Imperfectly formed or formulated.*

At Berkeley, that corporate sense of mission is as diffuse and **inchoate** as the resolute pluralism of California society.

indefeasible (adjective) *Not capable of or not liable to being annulled or voided or undone.*

Mr. Lindblom dislikes a doctrinaire attitude toward anything. He incessantly encourages the pragmatic approach to economics. It naturally follows that any reliance on absolutes, or any reference to **indefeasible** "rights" is unwarranted and anachronistic.

indigent (adjective) *Poor; impoverished.*

Señora Cubela begged him to stay and eat something, quietly convinced that so distinguished a visitor would not share a meal in such **indigent** surroundings.

indite (verb) *To write, compose; to set down in writing.*

Fleetwood had been designated to give the first toast, and he had gone out of his way to **indite** a few sentences the meaning of which he knew would be understood by not more than a dozen of the hundred guests there.

individuation (noun) *The process by which individuals in society become differentiated from one another.*

The kind of community Nisbet told us we all needed, and the kind that now Reich enjoins upon us, is inconceivable in the absence of **individuation;** and the individual is what happens when the state ceases to be taken for granted as the necessary instrument for human progress.

indolence (noun) *Laziness; a failure to accept responsibility.*

Children need to feel at a very early age the whiplash of **indolence:** long dull lives washing dishes and seeing television movies of non–Third World countries such as Japan and West Germany with thriving populations.

ineffaceably (adverb) *In a manner impossible to deny or erase.*

It becomes relevant here to bear in mind that Clare Boothe Luce was always, necessarily, **ineffaceably,** a very attractive woman, no matter how hard she strove to make a theoretical cultural case forbidding any distinction between men and women.

ineluctable (adjective) *Not to be avoided, changed, or resisted.*

The loose-jointedness of their mode leaves the revolutionists in a frame of mind at once romantic and diffuse, and the rest of us without the great weapon available to King Canute, who was able to contrive what would nowadays be called a Confrontation between the **ineluctable** laws of nature and the superstitions of his subjects.

inept (adjective) *Lacking skill or aptitude for a particular role or task.*

A man gifted in research is not thereby gifted in the art of transmitting to the pupil his knowledge. This is periodically brought to mind in widespread student resentment at the retention by many universities of scholars who, while often distinguished in research, are miserably **inept** in teaching.

ineradicable (adjective) *Incapable of being gotten rid of completely.*

His scientific intelligence taught him that facts, among them those that had to do with (**ineradicable**? Was this defective loyalty to Marx-Lenin?) human appetites cannot be denied by ideological asseverations.

inertia (noun) *Indisposition to motion, exertion, or action; inertness.*

For many teachers the prospect of commuting to disagreeable sections of the city, to grapple with **inertia**, indiscipline, and hostility, is not what they had in mind at all when deciding to teach.

inexorable (adjective) *Not to be persuaded or moved by entreaty or prayer.*

The wisdom and indispensability of government action to regulate economy becomes the **inexorable** next step.

ingratiation (noun) *The act of winning favor; the process of insinuating oneself in the good graces of another.*

Mrs. Thatcher's speech was a tribute to her natural eloquence and to her formidable powers of **ingratiation.** Mostly it was a Special Relations speech about the enduring friendship of the two great English-speaking powers.

inhere (verb) *To be a fixed element or attribute of; belong.*

States are amoral institutions. In a "state" **inheres** the authority to preserve itself.

inimical (adjective) *Injurious; unfriendly to; harmful.*

The resistance to private-sector enterprise as **inimical** to abstract democracy is thoroughly ingrained in many who think themselves especially sensitive in their understanding.

iniquitous (adjective) *Sinful; evil; wrongful.*

There were those who, reviewing the work of Owen Lattimore, which included eleven days of interrogation by the chief counsel of a Senate committee, came to certain conclusions about him that Tom Wicker suggests were surrealistic at best, **iniquitous** at worst.

iniquitously (adverb) *Wickedly; sinfully.*

Molotov delivered a speech on the subject of the **iniquitously** close relationship between the U.S. and Japan.

in medias res (adverb; Lat.) *Into the thick of it.*

Even then, blissfully distracted, he found himself wondering, *in medias res:* Would his future duties require him to . . . seduce women routinely?

insouciance (noun) *Lighthearted unconcern; nonchalance.*

The refrain on the matter of wealth was widespread, the popular corollary of which was to reason on to **insouciance** with respect to poverty as (Ann Davidon, *Philadelphia Inquirer*) for instance: "But there is something rather beguiling and even enviable about this overdriven patrician and his way of life. Perhaps it is his apparently blithe blindness to most of the world's miseries."

insularity (noun) *Narrow-mindedness; detachment; isolation; provincialism.*

But Mr. Salinas has gradually eased Mexico away from a protectionism that represented at once socialist **insularity** and yanqui xenophobia.

insurrectionary (adjective) *Relating to or constituting an act or instance of revolting against civil authority or against an established government.*

But there was another movement, not properly **insurrectionary** but totally hostile to apartheid. The Inkatha movement is as large as that of the African National Congress, but its leaders were different.

intellection (noun) *Exercise of the intellect; reasoning, cognition, apprehension; a specific act of the intellect.*

We believe that millenniums of **intellection** have served an objective purpose. Certain problems have been disposed of.

intercredal (adjective) *Pertaining to conversations or exchanges between members of different faiths.*

The liberals' implicit premise is that **intercredal** dialogues are what one has with Communists, not conservatives, in relationship with whom normal laws of civilized discourse are suspended.

interloper (noun) *An unlawful intruder on a property or sphere of action; one that interferes or thrusts himself in wrongfully or officiously.*

I do not deny, and do not regret, that the general tendency of an opinion journal is to be particularly critical of any politician one considers as an **interloper** in one's own party.

internecine (adjective) *Mutually damaging; wounding.*

Stalin had singular historical problems to confront, from the **internecine** question of succession after the death of Lenin, to the dogged resistance of the kulak class, to the war by Hitler.

interposition (noun) *The actions of a state whereby its sovereignty is placed between its citizens and the federal government.*

I have a dream that one day the state of Alabama, whose governor's lips are presently dripping with the words of **interposition** and nullification, will be transformed.

interstice (noun) *A space, usually little, that intervenes between solid matter.*

Under Stalin, a list long but not indefinitely long was drawn up of prohibited activities. Anything not prohibited could be engaged in. That left little **interstices** within which to maneuver.

interstitial (adjective) *Coming in the small narrow spaces between the principal parts.*

Professor Donald MacKay is a physicist and a Christian. The remarkable exchange between him and Professor B. F. Skinner I present here with **interstitial** comment because what both men say merits more reflection than the pace of their spoken exchange permits.

intone (verb) *To utter in musical or prolonged tones; recite in singing tones or in a monotone.*

Black sternly discoursed on the illogic and immorality of the United States getting involved in a European war, recapitulating the phrases and paragraphs he had so often heard his father so earnestly **intone**.

intractable (adjective) *Unmovable; inflexible; difficult to lead.*

Is the Brezhnev doctrine really dead if the retreat from Afghanistan is nothing more than an unprofitable collision with a major and **intractable** force?

intransigence (noun) *Refusal to compromise, to come to an agreement or a reconciliation.*

Mr. Bush having asked Congress for a resolution backing a military response in the Gulf should Saddam Hussein persevere in **intransigence,** a distinction crystallizes. A very important distinction.

intrinsic (adjective) *Belonging to the inmost constitution or essential nature of a thing.*

The fact of discrimination in America against the Negro is of no more **intrinsic** concern to the Communists than the fact of discrimination against the Jews in Soviet Russia is of concern to them.

intrinsically (adverb) *Inherently; having to do with its own nature, property.*

Now the idea of reinstating the IRA for everybody is **intrinsically** appealing. Any tax modification that reduces taxes on savings is appealing.

intuit (verb) *To know or apprehend directly.*

Prosecutor Neely at this point **intuited** what Smith's strategy was.

inure (verb) *To come into operation; flow to; become operative; accrue.*

Those who do not enroll in the program do not make the payments, but neither do the benefits **inure** to them.

invective (noun) *Denunciatory or abusive language; vituperation.*

"You, by not using your donkey brain—excuse me, donkey," Beria spoke now in a voice of exaggerated deference,—"excuse me, donkey, for insulting your brain by comparing it with Bolgin's!" The **invective** lasted a full ten minutes before Beria sat down.

inveigh (verb) *To protest, in a dogged way; to make vehement, protracted objection.*

One day Castro stormed into a radio station, seizing the microphone and **inveighing** against Batista and praising freedom and democracy and social justice and anti-imperialism for a full ten minutes while his companions kept watch for the police.

invidious (adjective) *Detrimental to reputation, designed to denigrate.*

It is not intended as ethnically **invidious** to remark that history shows a propensity for violence in Latin America.

invidiously (adverb) *Intending to be critical; at the expense of.*

(WFB speaking of Roy Cohn) He shows his adamant loyalty to the FBI, well-sheltered contempt for the character of Martin Luther King, and scorn for hypocritical comparative judgments, he accuses the accuser, and he ends with a mom-and-pop defense of a favorite government agency. I say this, by the way, **invidiously.**

involuted (adjective) *Of an involved or complicated nature; abstruse, intricate.*

Recently Mr. Sargent Shriver said, "I am delighted to be in any cathedral where Mr. Adam Clayton Powell, Jr., is in the pulpit." Here is an **involuted** form of racism. It is short for: "Even though I know that Adam Clayton Powell, Jr., is a demagogue, whose power and reputation have been built on hatred between the races, I recognize he is a Black leader, and must treat him as though he were a qualified object of universal admiration."

ipso facto (adverb; Lat.) *By the very nature of the case.*

I do not mean to imply that simply because my viewpoint was not energetically circularized, the Council proved itself *ipso facto* ineffective.

irredentism (noun) *A claim by a nation to land that formerly belonged to it.*

A few miles to the west, the disorder and the killings go on in Ulster and Ireland, over the dogged question of self-rule: Ulster wants to hold on to its independence as a part of Great Britain, substantial elements within Ireland want **irredentism.**

irredentist (adjective) *Having to do with the claim by a nation to lands that once belonged to it.*

While formally going along with Peking in its insistence of sovereignty, we maintained, in effect, diplomatic representation in Taiwan. Meanwhile, the graduated liberal reforms of Chiang Ching-kuo combined with the industry and energy of the people of Taiwan to nurture an evolutionized super-minipower. And direct **irredentist** pressure from the mainland lessened.

irreducible (adjective) *Impossible to simplify or make easier or clearer; impossible to make less or smaller.*

And one has therefore to pause before proceeding to hold every Iraqi responsible for the crimes of Saddam Hussein and those front-line sadists who disgraced the **irreducible** maxims of human decency.

irruption (noun) *A sudden, violent, or forcible entry; a rushing or bursting in; a sudden or violent invasion.*

The question the white community faces, then, is whether the claims of civilization supersede those of universal suffrage. The British clearly believed they did when they acted to suppress the **irruption** in Kenya in 1952.

J

Jacobinical (adjective) *Of or relating to violent or revolutionary political extremism.*

At Columbia, Mr. Allard Lowenstein was hooted down and literally silenced for defending the right of Professor Herman Kahn to speak unmolested, and faculty members in that audience countenanced and even egged on the **Jacobinical** furies that ruled the crowd.

janissary (noun) *A member of a group of loyal or subservient troops, officials, or supporters.*

When it was finally clear that Carmine DeSapio had been thrown out by the ideological **janissaries** and the playboy reformers, there were still the conventional and highly poignant rituals to go through.

jape (noun) *Something designed to arouse amusement or laughter.*

"Oh," said Blacky, "so it was here that famous tryst took place?" Except that he was too stuffed with crème Chantilly, he'd have taken out his notebook, further to extend the historical **jape.**

jejune (adjective) *Devoid of substance, interest, significance.*

One of Edgar Smith's editorial contributions to the *Times* on prison reform had come out embarrassingly **jejune.**

jeremiad (noun) *A lamenting and denunciatory complaint: a dolorous tirade.*

Soaring taxes, inadequate police protection, irregular garbage collection, traffic congestion, the scarcity of low-cost housing: Great **jeremiads** can be written on each of these major deprivations which underwrite such a categorical disillusion as Mr. Richard Whalen's.

jocularity (noun) *Sense of fun; mirthfulness.*

Pano took the rest of his beer slowly. All the usual **jocularity** faded from his face.

junket (verb) *To travel as a congressman or public official at public expense, ostensibly on business, actually on a pleasure trip.*

Members of the judiciary do not send a million letters without postage, do not **junket** around the world, do not get free massages or whatever in the exercise room of the House of Representatives.

juridical (adjective) *Of or relating to law in general or to jurisprudence.*

A call by the President for a declaration of war last November would have passed Congress overwhelmingly and, you betcha, with Senator Kennedy voting in favor. The declaration having passed, the **juridical** house is now in order. Not only the impounding of funds, which the President managed under an old law, but much more.

juxtapose (verb) *Place side by side.*

The device was to contrive wisps of frivolous conversation, à la *The Women*, and **juxtapose** them with horror stories from the Vietnamese battlefront (get it?), so as to effect a Stendhalian contrast that would Arouse the Conscience of Versailles.

K

kedge (verb) *To dig an anchor in securely.*

Mr. Rockefeller's composure, though temporarily adrift, quickly **kedged** up in that splendid self-assurance of investigating panel chairmen.

kinetic (adjective) *Supplying motive force; energizing, dynamic.*

The conclusions of Professor Louis Hartz of Harvard are both historical and philosophical. There never was a sure-enough conservatism in America, he maintains, the American experience having been dynamic, revolutionary, pragmatic, **kinetic.**

kite (verb) *To get money or credit by a kite, a check drawn against uncollected funds in a bank account; to create a false bank balance by manipulating deposit accounts.*

Excepting the fiscal deficit, which presumably cannot be **kited** indefinitely, things could probably stumble along much as before without causing New York City to close down its doors.

knell (noun) *A death signal or passing bell; a warning of or a sound indicating the passing away of something.*

If we become identified with the point of view that the Social Security laws toll the **knell** of our departed freedoms, we will lose our credit at the bar of public opinion, or be dismissed as cultists of a terrestrial mystique.

L

lachrymal (adjective) *Marked by tears.*

Mrs. Chamorro, while making all the appropriate **lachrymal** sounds over the death of Enrique, has not overridden her Sandinista authorities to take charge of the investigation.

laconic (adjective) *Using or marked by the use of few words; terse, precise.*

Bertram Heath was a quiet, determined young man with the even-featured straight face and the steady brown eyes that signaled what was coming before the **laconic** twenty-year-old got out what was on his mind.

laconically (adverb) *With the use of few, rather than many, words; succinctly.*

Professor Galbraith, I'd be most grateful if you would answer my questions directly and **laconically.**

lacuna (noun) *The missing item, datum; the hole in someone's learning.*

Ten years ago a longtime friend of Sidney Hook confided in me the most wonderfully humanizing story of the **lacuna** in Hook's knowledge.

laggard (adjective) *Slow to act, to respond, to react.*

We are **laggard** on that [deterrent] front and we face a concrete problem in Europe given the tergiversation of Helmut Kohl on the modernizing of the remaining nuclear missiles in West Germany.

lagniappe (noun) *A gratuitous little gift, in any form, e.g., a free liqueur at a restaurant after dinner.*

Drugstore cowboys walk out into the street, hail the mob, and tell them to come in for free ice cream cones. That is how the Bush administration clearly understands Gorbachev's **lagniappe** when he offered to destroy 500 missiles, 2.5 percent of his inventory, reducing the threat to export glasnostian Bolshevism by a factor of nothing, these missiles having been redundant for years.

languorous (adjective) *Producing or tending to produce a state of the body or mind caused by exhaustion or disease and characterized by a weak, sluggish feeling.*

History adduces now and again a morally **languorous** pope who was awakened from his slumbers (and many more popes who slept through it all) by morally energetic laymen, preferably saints.

lapidary (adjective) *Having the elegance and precision associated with inscriptions on stone.*

To accept Mr. Simpson's thesis is to suppose that writers (and poets) always feel that the language of the moment is **lapidary,** never mind that, when detoxified, they proceed to make changes.

largesse (noun) *Liberality in giving, especially when attended by condescension.*

He felt positively ennobled by the proposed act of generosity, but also tender in the knowledge of whom he stood now to patronize with his **largesse.**

lasciviously (adverb) *Luxuriantly, wantonly.*

I had at the moment the campaign began no personal animus, certainly not a shred of that "personal disdain" which John Lindsay's biographer so **lasciviously** records.

latently (adverb) *Dormantly, but usually capable of being evoked, expressed, or brought to light.*

Why would it make for good politics to endorse the impression that the New York City police force is **latently** sympathetic with the brutality shown under stress by the Selma police force?

latitudinarianism (noun) *Broadmindedness; permissiveness.*

The feds shrewdly decided to try Harry Reems in Memphis, Tennessee, a venue not given to **latitudinarianism** in matters of obscenity.

leech (verb) *To fasten onto, as a leech; feed on the blood or substance of.*

I once contributed to the impression that Beame was ordinary, or rather leeched on it, at a speech where I remarked that Mr. Beame constantly stressed that he was educated by the City of New York, "which fact should be obvious," I said; and I am ashamed of it.

lèse majesté (noun; Fr.) *An offense against the sovereign; whence an indignity at the expense of the reigning authority.*

When Newt Gingrich took time off to insist that evasion of the reelection finance laws ought to apply not only to lowly congressmen but also to the Speaker of the House, he faced a barrage of shocked fraternity brothers unaccustomed to violations of the law of **lèse majesté.**

levity (noun) *Lacking in seriousness; a frivolity.*

"Not even you can talk that way about Comrade Beria. And this business of going to the British Embassy . . . I mean, Alistair, don't ever say such a thing, not even in **levity.**"

libertarian (adjective) *Pertaining to the political philosophy that stresses the absolute right of the individual to make his own decisions, unobstructed by the state.*

Conservatives raised on **libertarian** principles have long since remarked that any invasion of the sacred No Trespassing sign puts you on the slippery slope toward collectivist capitulation.

licentious (adjective) *Marked by the absence of legal or moral restraints; by lewdness; by neglect.*

Such discrepancies as the bigoted churchman, the protectionist free enterpriser, the provincial internationalist, the **licentious** moralist are all well-known anomalies.

licentiousness (noun) *The disregard of accepted standards of meaning, behavior, analysis.*

The terminological **licentiousness** of the day is very striking. In his book Paul Johnson quotes Castro as saying, "Of course we're a democratic society. We have a democracy every day, inasmuch as we're expressing the will of the people." It's that kind of wordplay which is the essence, as Orwell told us in another connection, of totalitarianism.

licit (adjective) *Legally or otherwise allowable; condonable.*

It is easy to imagine (and frightening to do so) the result of a refusal by the minority to abide by the **licit** authority of the majority.

limn (verb) *To become visible, traceable, detectable as to features or form.*

Young Jesús Ferrer, with his cosmopolitan background, his derring-do in the mountains, gradually **limned** into the consciousness of the press.

lineaments (noun) *An outline, feature, or contour of a body or figure; the distinguishing or characteristic feature of something immaterial.*

It was terribly clear from the visceral reactions of such people as Jackie Robinson that thousands of people were taking very special, even an acute, pleasure from believing that a sudden flash of light had exposed the **lineaments** of the wolf.

literati (noun) *The literate, educated class.*

What proved most curious is that there was a substantial lobby that night, among the **literati** of Louisville, for every position concerning the drug problem.

locus classicus (noun; Lat.) *A standard passage important for the elucidation of a word or subject.*

It can be argued by orthodox theologians that God prefers the sinner to the saint, always provided it is understood that overnight the sinner can, and in the past often has, become a saint. Augustine is the ***locus classicus.***

lodestar (noun) *The guiding force, star; the focus of attention, inspiration.*

Kissinger Associates would almost certainly not succeed as a partnership of 100 retired Foreign Service officers: The relationship to the **lodestar** becomes too attenuated.

logorrhea (noun) *Pathologically excessive and often incoherent talkativeness.*

That bit of **logorrhea** is a way of saying that the Founding Fathers were incompetent when they gave individual states, instead of just the federal government, the taxing power, because this federalist invitation to centrifugal disruption adds up to people being able to look Mario Cuomo in the face and say, "Raise taxes one more time, and we'll give you a forwarding address in Pennsylvania."

longueur (noun) *An overlong passage, made dull or tedious.*

The **longueurs** in Trudeau's "Doonesbury" are sometimes almost teasingly didactic.

loquacious (adjective) *Given to excessive talking.*

Sometimes we spend as much as a half hour in conversation. He is, oddly, **loquacious,** and enjoys our intercourse.

lotus (noun) *The mythical Greek fruit, the eating of which induced torpid satisfaction, pleasure, forgetfulness of duty.*

The mood is out there, and we are tasting the **lotus** in the green pastures of peace.

lubricity (noun) *Tendency to sexual stimulation; salacious.*

Blackford remonstrated every now and then when Anthony's **lubricity** got out of hand. "You are like a lot of Englishmen," Blackford once told Anthony. "They learn about sex later than we do and freeze into a Freudian first gear whenever anything remotely suggestive comes up."

lucidity (noun) *The quality or state of being clear to the understanding; readily intelligible; lacking ambiguity.*

"You have, sometimes, a terribly obscure way of expressing yourself, a difficulty you may have noticed that never afflicted my mentor, Jane Austen, who had no problem in expressing thoughts no matter how subtle, with unambiguous **lucidity.**"

lucubrate (verb) *To discourse learnedly in writing.*

Under the Eisenhower program, one could **lucubrate** over constitutional rights and freedoms and forever abandon captured American soldiers.

Luddite (adjective) *Pertaining to the nineteenth-century movement that disapproved of labor-saving devices. Hence, opposed to technological progress.*

We, the government, will protect you—even as we protect bank depositors—against lawsuits the effect of which is to enrich the legal participants, protect nobody against a threat not yet perceived, and wrench the United States into a **Luddite** gear which, had such a thing happened two generations ago, would have been the equivalent of forbidding the flight of airplanes on the grounds that one of them would lose its wings and fall on Aunt Minnie.

Luddite

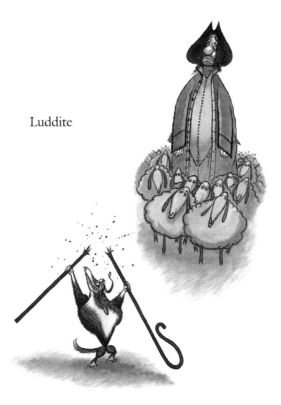

lugubrious (adjective) *Mournful, sad, lachrymose.*

Jean-François Revel gave many **lugubrious** examples of the working of the Western mind.

lumpen (adjective) *Pertaining to an amorphous group of dispossessed and uprooted individuals set off by their inferior status from the economic and social class with which they are identified, or to a geographical area backward and undistinguished.*

Several years ago I wrote in this space that the Soviet Union, were it deprived of its strategic nuclear weapons, would become nothing much more than a vast **lumpen** territorial mass, something on the order of a north India.

lurid (adjective) *Gruesome; horrifying; causing shock or horror.*

The documents they were given to read were in many respects **lurid,** melodramatic—preposterous even, so their exchanges were not always in the diapasonal mode when one of the young CIA agents would interrupt his reading to make a comment or ask a question.

M

Machiavellian (adjective) *Crafty, deceitful; of, like, or characterized by the political principles and methods of expediency, craftiness, and duplicity advocated in Niccolò Machiavelli's book* The Prince.

The **Machiavellian** principle that you do not fool with the prince unless you are prepared to kill him was never more clearly vindicated than in the current exercise.

machicolation (noun) *An opening for shooting or dropping missiles upon assailants attacking below.*

"After the next war," the Queen said cheerily, "when we shall all have exchanged hydrogen bombs, I should think these archives would be tremendously useful, since whoever is left over will be reduced to defending himself by the use of things like moats and **machicolations** and bows and arrows . . ."

maculation (noun) *Spot, stain, blemish.*

The new conservatives, many of whom go by the name of Modern Republicans, have not been very helpful. Their sin consists in permitting so many accretions, modifications, emendations, **maculations,** and qualifications that the original thing quite recedes from view.

magnanimous (adjective) *Generous, suggesting special inclinations to charity or philanthropy.*

Phil Donahue came up with an alternative suggestion that also commended itself to his audience—the Shah should undertake to return to Iran to face the punishment. (This **magnanimous** willingness to bring martyrdom to someone else recalls the wisecrack of 1939 to the effect that the British were prepared to fight to the last Frenchman.)

maladroitness (noun) *Lacking in shrewdness of execution, craft, or resourcefulness in coping with difficulty or danger.*

One can have no objections whatever to President Carter's mission, restricting our criticism to the **maladroitness** of its execution and the insufficiency of contingency planning.

malefactor (noun) *One who does ill toward another; evildoer.*

Whatever good they accomplished it can't be denied that they also did great harm, and that the principal **malefactor** was Senator Frank Church, who treated the hearings as a confessional.

malfeasance (noun) *The doing by a public officer under cover of authority of his office of something that is unwarranted, that he has contracted not to do, and that is legally unjustified and positively wrongful or contrary to law.*

Edward Bennett Williams pleads for action to deprive the Congress of the right to exercise its traditional power to expose crime and **malfeasance,** to forbid the police from tapping the telephones of putative criminals, to restrain detectives from interrogating suspects.

malleable (adjective) *Open to outside forces or influences; urging a change in position, viewpoint.*

The courts are less **malleable** than they were even for Roosevelt. The Supreme Court gave him problems, and he tried to pack it, and eventually, got himself a court that would go along.

malum in se (noun; Lat.) *An act that is evil or wrong from its own nature or by the natural law irrespective of statute.*

What the government of South Africa did is a nice example of the distinction between a *malum prohibitum* and a ***malum in se.*** It is legally wrong for a government to subsidize one particular political movement at the expense of another. It is not always morally wrong to do so.

malversation (noun) *Corrupt administration.*

The Seabury disclosures that brought Fusion to the fore are not to be confused with the routine **malversations** of public officials.

manifestly (adverb) *Made obvious by its own appearance; self-evidently.*

We are invited to believe that if John Tower participates in any of the activities engaged in by Alexander the Great, Napoleon and General Grant, he is **manifestly** unfit to serve.

manifesto (noun) *A public demonstration of intentions, motives, or views; a public statement of policy or opinion.*

Because liberalism has no definitive **manifesto,** one cannot say, prepared to back up the statement with unimpeachable authority, that such-and-such a man or measure is "liberal."

manifold (adjective) *Various; multiple; of many kinds.*

The following day Olga Kirov walked into the Cuban Embassy, explained that the Señorita Rincona was expecting her, and was admitted into the special reception area, heavily armed because of the **manifold** requirements associated with Fidel Castro's visit.

manumission (noun) *Formal emancipation from slavery.*

The dutiful Mr. Walter Cronkite closes his broadcast every night by citing the number of days in the infinitely prolonged negotiations having as their objective the hostages' release. The result of this kind of thing over a period of five months is that we are not one step closer to the **manumission** than we were on the fifth of last November.

mastodonic (adjective) *Something unusually, surrealistically large.*

But when you endeavor to shake the conviction that the **mastodonic** oil deposits that guard growlingly the outskirts of Bridgeport reflect the size of your own financial resources, a student at the University of Bridgeport displays amusement at my suggestion that it was neither factually nor symbolically correct that I was there to argue the case for the Buckley oil interest in Bridgeport, *über alles.*

matriculate (verb) *To become admitted to membership in a body, society, or institution.*

Blackford completed his application for graduate school rather listlessly; convinced, correctly, that he would never **matriculate** during this bellicose season.

matrix (noun) *A situation or surrounding substance within which something originates, develops, or is contained.*

She was to keep a sharp eye out for any student who inclined sufficiently toward the great Communist experiment, of which Russia was the **matrix,** to qualify for possible recruitment.

meliorative (adjective) *Resulting in or leading toward betterment.*

There is no guarantee behind the value of the policy taken out with a private insurance company, which is subject to the depredations of inflation unmitigated by **meliorative** political pressure.

metaphysical (adjective) *Beyond measurement; transcendent; supersensible.*

Those who rail against it do so for the most practical reason: They have not mastered its use. They strive for **metaphysical** formulations to justify their hidden little secret (sloth and fear).

metastasize (verb) *To spread to other parts of the body by metastasis; to change form or matter; to transform.*

And the possibility was also there to be considered that what happened between the judge and his associate wasn't seductive flirtation but something misinterpreted as such, growing grotesque in the imagination, sufficient to **metastasize** as an inclination to bestiality.

mete (verb) *To assign by measure; deal out; allot, apportion.*

Too many judges appear to have forgotten that the primary purpose of courts of justice is to assert the demands of the public order—by **meting** out convincing punishment to those who transgress against it.

meticulist (noun) *One who is extremely careful in his use of language, diction; a precise measurer.*

It hurt Governor Sununu, who is a **meticulist** in expression, to use a term inappropriate to his conduct.

mien (noun) *The air or bearing of a person, especially as expressive of mood or personality.*

Black's final instructor had obviously spent much time in England. He was a gray man, his **mien,** hair, face, suit, shirt.

miff (verb) *To offend; annoy.*

"Is it your guess," Ruth probed, "that Castro would shrug his shoulders if she got **miffed**?"

militate (verb) *To have weight or effect.*

The young graduate of Yale, the potential entrepreneur, must remember that money costs do not tally with social costs, and that therefore it is quite possible that the enterprise he is considering, regardless of its financial success, will **militate** against the social welfare.

mille-feuilles (noun; Fr.) *A light, layered pastry commonly called a Napoleon.*
The braised chicken and petits pois were fine, the claret excellent, the *mille-feuilles* sensational.

millenarian (noun) *The person who believes that perfection is coming for us down the line, for reasons biological, political, or theological.*
Paul Johnson: Broadly speaking, there are two types of people. One is the person who believes in God. The other is the type who says, "I don't believe in God. I don't believe in an afterlife. It's all nonsense. This life is the only one we've got, and we have to try to improve it, and I don't believe that human—"
WFB: The **millenarian**?
Johnson: Yes. "—I don't accept that human nature is permanently imperfect. It can be perfected."

mimetic (adjective) *Imitative.*
Wolfe: In domestic architecture there was constant guerrilla warfare and rebellions and so forth. But not in great public structures.
WFB: What does that tell us about the response of public men—this sort of **mimetic** response as against the relative individualism of the consumer?
Wolfe: In this country, in the midst of what could certainly be called the American Century, we remain the most obedient in matters of the arts—we remain the most obedient little colonial subjects of Europe.

mirabile dictu (adverb; Lat.) *"Wonder to relate"; incredible.*
Here is a question for which, *mirabile dictu,* I do not have the answer. It is: How much freedom should a college student be given to say or to write what he wishes?

miscegenetic (adjective) *Having to do with the mixture of the races.*
The new policy would say to the Soviet Union: Look, the big dream—

mimetic

the ideological conquest of the world—isn't going to happen. Not only is it not going to happen, other things aren't going to happen—namely a permanent, **miscegenetic** annexation of Eastern Europe by you. So let's make a deal.

miscible (adjective) *Capable of mixing in any ratio without separation of two phases.*

It is a pity that the useless word "equality" ever got into the act, because one cannot in the nature of things make "equal" that which is not the same. You can play around with other words if you wish—fungible? No, the sexes aren't fungible. **Miscible?** Yes: but miscible elements retain their identity.

miscreant (noun) *One who behaves criminally or viciously.*

That spirit looks upon a nuclear missile not only as a ferule with which to beat the enemy and native **miscreants,** but as a badge of high office.

misogynist (noun) *One who hates women.*

Those who believe that a case for differences between the two can be plausibly made might have no trouble suppressing or expelling the student pornographer, but would pause over taking action against the student racist or homophobe or **misogynist** or whatever.

mollify (verb) *To quiet; soothe; lessen.*

Do I understand you, Mr. Reagan, to say that the actual role attempted by, say, President Johnson during the riots of his administration might have exacerbated the situation rather than helped to **mollify** it?

mollifying (adjective) *Making more agreeable; conciliatory; soothing.*

I have seen a variety of official answers to correspondents of Mr. Ober's general persuasion. Replies were **mollifying** in tone, but firm, and abundant in phrases like "freedom of speech" and "the great traditions of academic freedom."

monetize (verb) *To coin into money.*

There is a tale (I think it was Ring Lardner's) of an old prospector who shrinks from the attendant complexities and unpleasantness of mining and **monetizing** a rich deposit of gold he has come upon.

monitory (adjective) *Warning; admonitory.*

When the censor, at the special request of the Russian-Cuban interpreter, promised a quick reading of the letter to Major Kirov from his wife, he checked his files routinely, and spotted the **monitory** marking.

moot (adjective) *Rendered irrelevant by circumstances; no longer of practical significance.*

Suddenly we discover that the FBI knows somebody or some people who have seen John Tower under the influence; but, in any event, the whole question became **moot** when he made his public pledge to give up drinking altogether, if confirmed.

mordant (adjective) *Biting or caustic in thought, manner, or style; incisive; keen.*

Through it all, Smith had managed to put forward his case in an almost disinterested perspective. He was by turns **mordant,** judicious, inquisitive, impudent, amused.

moribund (adjective) *Deathly; about to die; having to do with death.*

When there was someone else in the room on unrelated business, Castro and Tamayo would satisfy themselves, after the **moribund** dialogue, with an oblique cross-glance, an exchanged wink.

morphological (adjective) *Of, relating to, or concerned with form or structure.*
The state can rule, but it cannot command loyalty, let alone effect **morphological** changes in human nature.

morphology (noun) *The study of the nature of a word, thought, movement, including its causes and its composition.*
Firing Line continued to deal with much else, but, inevitably, spent time in the sixties on The Sixties: on its culture, its **morphology,** and its implications.

mortification (noun) *The subjection and denial of bodily passions and appetites by abstinence or self-inflicted pain or discomfort.*
When he decided to enter the monastery, he decided, as a novitiate, to impose upon himself the intellectual **mortification** of learning physics.

mugwumpery (noun) *The views and practices of a mugwump, one who withdraws his support from a political group or organization: a regular member who bolts a party and adopts an independent position.*
Lindsay's biographer does not know how to handle the problem. On the one hand, Lindsay's transcendence of Republicanism must be presented as a statesmanlike projection of true Republican principle. On the other, a touch of **mugwumpery** is always charming.

mulct (verb) *To leach from, gather up from, drain.*
In order for a nation to guard the common defense or look after the unfortunate, there has to be a certain residue. That residue can be **mulcted** from the masses, as in the Soviet Union, leaving them without the essential freedoms to engage in commerce or to blunt the sharp edges of life, or it can come out of what can reasonably be called a "surplus."

multicentrist (noun) *Those who hold that attachments to many positions, political, social, cultural, are educationally advanced.*
Having dealt with Islamic codes on women, the pilgrims in search of better ideas than those of our own culture can study the attitudes of others toward homosexuality, since homophobia is one of the central targets of the **multicentrists.**

multifarious (adjective) *Many and various; diverse.*

Castro liked it when his intimates joined him in exploring the **multi-farious** reefs around Cuba.

munificent (adjective) *Very liberal in giving or bestowing; lavish; characterized by great liberality or generosity.*

Many people come to New York because they are deluded, at least momentarily, into believing the myth of New York's **munificent** opportunities.

munificently (adverb) *Liberally, with lavish generosity.*

Big social thinkers assume that any proposal is emasculated that doesn't call for federal funding on a very large scale. What the Bennet school of criticism wishes to see in national service is a full-scale war against poverty. Again; federal programs **munificently** funded.

muse (noun) *The creative spirit of an individual, the source of his inspiration.*

I would sooner risk the displeasure of a voter than I would that of my **muse,** who is more demanding.

mutatis mutandis (adverb; Lat.) *The necessary changes having been made.*

How many Americans, reflecting on the misuse of a government limousine, have asked themselves whether they should be fired by their employers because every now and again they use a postage stamp from the office supply to mail a personal letter? *Mutatis mutandis,* they might say to themselves, that is the equivalent of misusing a government limousine, if you are chief of staff of the White House.

mycology (noun) *The properties and life phenomena exhibited by a fungus, fungus type, or fungus group—the study of mushrooms.*

How many things Whittaker Chambers wanted to write about! Mushrooms, for one thing. Some gentleman had recently published a ten-dollar book on **mycology,** heaping scorn on one of Chambers's most beloved species of toadstools.

N

nabob (noun) *An important character, whether by reason of heredity, power, or wealth.*

Henry Kissinger has an inclination to know who are the movers and shakers. To suggest that this is on the order of a movie starlet wanting to know the industry's **nabobs** is entirely to misunderstand the point.

naïf (noun) *A naïve person.*

Within ten minutes Tucker knew he was dealing, in the case of the gook, with a total **naïf.** The Russian's background, on the other hand, was considerable.

nascent (adjective) *Aborning; about to be.*

I had persuaded Steve Allen in the course of a discursive afternoon that the logic of his adamant stand against nuclear weapons committed him to backing a preemptive strike against the **nascent** nuclear-bomb facilities of Red China (as we used to call it).

necromancy (noun) *Black magic; sorcery; the practice of claiming to foretell the future by alleged communication with the dead.*

When you raise taxes, you raise taxes. When you forecast spending decreases, you are engaged in **necromancy.**

nefarious (adjective) *Disreputable; unethical; detestable.*

The feds charge insider trading and a number of other activities, some of them **nefarious,** some of them—well, that is one of the reasons so many people are interested in Mr. Milken.

nepotistically (adverb) *Characterized by nepotism, favoritism shown to relatives.*

It had already been rumored that Blackford's selection to fly the new fighter had been **nepotistically** contrived.

nescience (noun) *The belief that nothing is establishable, provable.*

How is it that the president of a distinguished and cosmopolitan university tells us that God alone knows when human life begins? If you penetrate this rhetorical formulation, you have a dimly obscured invitation to **nescience.** "God alone knows" is the safest way to say, "That-is-unknowable." Inasmuch as God is not invited to teach a regular course at Yale, Mr. Giamatti is saying in effect that the search for the answer to "When does life begin?" should be abandoned—because no one can tell.

nescient (adjective) *From nescience, the doctine that nothing is truly knowable.*
 I intended to call my little book "The Revolt Against the Masses,"
 because I thought I saw on the social horizon in America signs of a disposition to reject the **nescient** aimlessness Ortega y Gasset had diagnosed.

nether (adjective) *Situated down or below; lying beneath or in the lower part.*
 The conservative should shake loose from his disposition to reject out
 of hand any gesture in the direction of acknowledging different orders
 of citizenship. That line of demarcation should exist, among other reasons, in order to prompt those on the **nether** side to traverse it.

nexus (noun) *Connection, interconnection, tie, link.*
 Reason, conscience, and self-restraint are all that we have to rely upon,

the burden resting on those who postulate a **nexus** between a sane position and an insane extension of it to make their demonstration.

noblesse oblige (noun; Fr.) *The inferred obligation of people of high rank or social position to behave nobly or kindly toward others.*

But individual employers, acting on an impulse of *noblesse oblige,* aren't to be confused with the government, which must never discriminate in its own hiring practices.

nomenclature (noun) *A vocabulary associated with an art, or science, or discipline.*

Rolando had not got used to the brevity of revolutionary **nomenclature** and found it difficult to say *"Buenas noches, Paco"* to a man twice his age.

nomenklatura (noun) *The elite within the Soviet bureaucracy.*

Well there is no doubt they have considerable influence—the **nomenklatura,** the KGB, the military—but I ask you to imagine how much worse off the Soviet Union would be without Gorbachev.

non grata (adjective; Lat.) *Not approved; unwelcome.*

Others convey to the student who majors in sociology the definite impression that at best religion is *non grata* to the department, at worst it is the subject of relentless attack.

nonplussed (verb) *To cause to be at a loss as to what to say, think, or do.*

I put the question to the biographer of Mr. Hoover, Dr. George Nash the distinguished historian. He **nonplussed** me by telling me that he was himself **nonplussed.** So much so that he went to the archives and dug up the first one hundred communications sent to President Hoover after he left the White House.

nuance (noun) *A subtle or slight degree of difference as in meaning, color, or tone.*

She discovered that in his subtle way, the slim young man with no trace of beard, a light sprinkle of faded freckles reaching from his nose to his hair, was quick to grasp **nuance** and to expand and improvise on subjects only tangentially touched upon.

nuanced (adjective) *Given to slight, delicate, subtle degrees of meaning, explanation, analysis.*

Firing Line is a **nuanced** program, and a thorough knowledge of English is required to do justice to subtle thought.

nugatory (adjective) *Trifling; of little importance.*

It has always seemed to me that the correct balance of police power and individual rights should reflect the crime rate. The interdiction by the airlines of terrorist weapons, conducted at the expense of every American who steps foot on an airplane, can be demonstrated statistically to be **nugatory** in its accomplishments.

numinous (adjective) *Divine, magical.*

Rosalyn Tureck sits down and pulls out that talismanic handkerchief, the fondling of which precedes the contact of her **numinous** fingers with the keyboard.

O

obduracy (noun) *The quality or state of being hard or resistant.*

I am not talking about someone who has familiarized himself sufficiently with the great scientific impasses that at various stages in the struggle to achieve the bomb have constituted roadblocks of historical **obduracy.**

obeisance (noun) *A movement of the body or other gesture made in token of respect or submission.*

Blackford rose, walked gravely to the lectern, and bowed with the faintly wooden truncation that becomes those ill at ease with the filigreed lengths of native **obeisances,** first to the Queen, then to the Archbishop.

objurgation (noun) *An act of decrying vehemently; castigation with harsh or violent language; harsh or violent reproof.*

Mrs. Gunning had, as chief organizer of the Parents and Taxpayers Association, been widely denounced, that being the cant **objurgation,** as an enemy of the Public Schools.

oblation (noun) *Something offered or presented in worship or sacred service.*

I tell about the monk—the ex-circus hand—who, having no relevant skills, and having observed the artful **oblations** rendered by his brothers on the Feast Day of the Virgin, was spotted late that night, standing before her statue juggling his five weatherbeaten circus balls.

obloquy (noun) *A strongly and often intemperately condemnatory utterance; defamatory or calumnious language; abusive or slanderous reprehension.*

After an elaborate exposition of the problem, he would pronounce sentence. This ranged from disqualification, on the lenient days, to a terrible warning to which, of course, was attached public **obloquy.**

obsequious (adjective) *Fawning; servile; sycophantic.*

Even if one accepted Castro's figures, the progress in his country cannot match the progress in other Caribbean nations, so what is there to celebrate, save the hope that the day will come when the mere mention of Castro's name calls to mind not only massive torture, political prisoners and a docile, **obsequious** press, but also a lifeless society, fallen behind in general welfare.

obsequy (noun) *Gesture of reverence, or piety, or deference, usually toward the dead.*

And poor Senator Gore! He was accused by properly indignant New York Jews of "pandering" to the Jewish vote by his near-sacramental **obsequies** to whatever Tel Aviv's policy was five minutes ago.

obstreperous (adjective) *Stubbornly defiant; resisting control or restraint, often with a show of noisy disorder.*

Mike Wallace introduces Randolph Churchill as an "irascible snob." Now for all I know, that is just what Mr. Churchill is; but this is not the way to introduce one's guests, not even **obstreperous** conservative guests.

obtrude (verb) *To thrust out; push forward.*

"Your husband is at San Cristóbal," the interpreter said, a smile **obtruding** her creased face.

obverse (noun) *The other, opposite side.*

The business of finding twelve jurors in Washington, D.C., who so to speak never heard of Colonel Oliver North assumes ludicrous proportions, something like the **obverse** of Diogenes' search for an honest man.

ochlocracy (noun) *Government by the mob; mob rule.*

She found it increasingly easy to achieve informality—to the dismay of her impossibly punctilious husband who desired **ochlocracy** abroad but, at home, to be paid homage even by the baboons at the zoo.

oenophile (noun) *A lover or connoisseur of wine.*

Blackford wondered where the **oenophiles'** journals were and thought Ellison must be a real sport to pass himself off as a winetaster, working in the sunkissed vineyards of Washington, D.C.

oeuvre (noun; Fr.) *Usually, the sum of an artist's lifework.*

Blackford was showing off here, as he wished Sally to know that he knew where Mr. Knightley and Miss Woodhouse had figured in Miss Austen's *oeuvre.*

officious (adjective) *Showing bureaucratic attention; offering unnecessary and perhaps unwanted advice and services.*

She was surprised when, at the airport in Mexico, a middle-aged man, portly and **officious** (he bellowed out instructions to the porter who accompanied him), approached her at the gate of her flight, his diplomatic badge, pinned conspicuously above his breast pocket, permitting him into the inspection compound.

oleaginous (adjective) *Unctuous; oily; affected.*

On the second evening of his state visit in Moscow, Fidel Castro had been carried away by an **oleaginous** toast in his honor delivered by Soviet President Leonid Brezhnev.

oligarch (noun) *The controlling member of a party or state.*

Being able to vote is no more to have realized freedom than being able to read is to have realized wisdom. Reasonable limitations upon the vote are not recommended exclusively by tyrants or **oligarchs** (was Jefferson either?).

oligopolistically (adverb) *In the manner of a small group of agents who control the market.*

(Speaking of OPEC) Thirteen governments **oligopolistically** took hold of a great reservoir of the supply of oil and quadrupled its prices overnight.

ombudsman (noun) *One who investigates complaints, as from consumers, reports findings, and assists in achieving fair settlements.*

Should the federal government pay **ombudsmen** who would stand at the door of the public library, prepared to extract from the mainframe the information desired by the curious citizen?

omnibus (adjective) *Of, relating to, or providing for many things at once.*

What we have is a great blur, an **omnibus** bill that goes everywhere from collecting taxes on tips at hamburger stands, to one that clips you extra on a phone call, to one that immobilizes one or another business merger because of changes in tax scheduling.

omnicompetent (adjective) *Well qualified in all respects.*

That morning Rufus had arrived at the safe house in London looking old, but not for that reason less than **omnicompetent.**

ontological (adjective) *Of or relating to being or existence.*

The persistent misuse of the word democracy reflects either an ignorance of its **ontological** emptiness; or (and is this not the logical derivative of the ignorance?), the pathetic attempt to endow it with substantive meaning.

onus (noun) *Something (as a task, duty, responsibility) that involves considerable difficulty or annoyance; a burden.*

The probabilities are small that the cost of any modern government will reduce: which puts the **onus** back on the private sector to generate additional revenues, and ends us back with the question: Is the scarcity of public funds the major problem?

opera (noun; Lat.) *Plural of opus, a set of compositions usually numbered in order of issue.*

Arthur Schlesinger, Jr., for a decade or so was more or less ex officio in charge of disdaining my *opera* and writing the score for others on just how this was to be done.

opéra-bouffe (adjective; Fr.) *Apt for a light comic opera characterized by parody or burlesque.*

"I persuaded a friend of mine from M.I.T. to go see the old gentleman.

They hit it off and my friend is now hired," said Blackford with a feigned air of *opéra-bouffe* secretiveness.

opine (verb) *To give a formal opinion about.*

Pundits need to **opine** on developments in China while fearing that what we write on Monday will be obsolete on Tuesday.

opprobrium (noun) *Public or known disgrace or ill fame that ordinarily follows from conduct considered grossly wrong or vicious.*

There are circumstances when the minority can lay claim to preeminent political authority, without bringing down upon its head the moral **opprobrium** of just men.

organon (noun) *An instrument for acquiring knowledge, specifically a body of methodological doctrine comprising principles for scientific or philosophic procedure or investigations.*

Those liberating perceptions Norman Mailer has been wrestling to formulate for lo these many years are like the purloined letter, lying about loose in the principles and premises, the **organon,** of the movement the Left finds it so fashionable to ridicule.

orotund (adjective) *Unduly strong in delivery or style.*

"You and your goddam . . . continence. I guess after graduation you'll go into training for the Graduate Engineering School lacrosse team and inflict on the next guy the necessity to go out into the wild night, in search of a normal room, with normal people, and normal supplies of the normal vices of this world."

Johnny got **orotund** when he was tight, and Blackford smiled at the familiar chiding.

ostracism (noun) *The exclusion by general consent from common privilege or social acceptance.*

What should happen is what should have happened when martial law was declared in Poland: a total economic, social, and cultural **ostracism** of the Soviet Union.

oxymoronic (adjective) *Relating to a combination for epigrammatic effect of contradictory or incongruous words.*

Michael Harrington's **oxymoronic** formulation—"coercion in favor of capitalists"—reminds us of the fashionable jargon in the commodity markets of the left (alas, not greatly changed).

oxymoronic

P

paean (noun) *A fervent expression of joy or praise.*

Alice wrote poetry, and her poetry included **paeans** to the Soviet state and its leaders, though she had had on more than one occasion to face the metrical choice either of substituting the name of a new leader in the place of the name that figured in her original lines but was now exposed as having been treasonable, or toss the poem away.

palliative (noun) *Something that moderates the intensity of.*

Bowman and Bach's **palliatives** are mild by comparison with some of their brethren textbook writers who have molded the attitudes of so many students.

pallid (adjective) *Lacking brightness or intensity.*

The truly extraordinary feature of our time isn't the faithlessness of the Western people; it is their utter, total ignorance of the Christian religion. They travel to Rishikesh to listen to **pallid** seventh-hand imitations of thoughts and words they never knew existed.

palpably (adverb) *Obviously; transparently; perceptibly.*

She moved, for the first year or so, **palpably** under a shadow and it wasn't until the end of the spring term that her irrepressibly buoyant roommate unearthed the cause of Sally's melancholy and set out to do something about it.

pander (verb) *To truckle to someone's desires, usually disreputable — e.g., lust, greed, power hunger.*

Would it be possible to institute death as the penalty for drug merchants? Would the court prohibit the execution of drug merchants who had **pandered** to minors?

parabolically (adverb) *Expressed in the manner of a parable or figure; allegorically.*

It was easy to deny the rumor, that I had flown to Phoenix, Arizona, a few weeks earlier, there to meet with Barry Goldwater and Mrs. Clare Boothe Luce, since it was not true, not even **parabolically.**

paradigm (noun) *An idealistic model.*

But Lenin had working for him not only the excitement of throwing over a dynasty, but of remaking a state around an ideological **paradigm** that excited everyone by its call to equality.

paralogism (noun) *Reasoning contrary to the rules of logic; a faulty argument.*

This is the critical **paralogism** in the Choicers' line of argument. What they should be saying is that the woman's right to abort is superior to the right of the fetus to live.

paralogist (noun) *One who uses reasoning that begs the question; one who uses a reasoning contrary to logical rules or formulas.*

A good debater is not necessarily an effective vote-getter: you can find a hole in your opponent's argument and thrill at the crystallization of a truth wrung out from a bloody dialogue—which may warm only you and your muse, while the smiling **paralogist** has made votes by the tens of thousands.

parlous (adjective) *Characterized by uncertainty; fraught with danger or risk; attended with peril.*

The situation in South Africa during the past, **parlous** years isn't as vivid seen through the serene eyes of a lecturer at the Kennedy School at Harvard as it has been, and continues to be, for the white South African.

parricide (noun) *The act of killing one's father.*

Now, "fraternity" is a word one needs to pause over, inasmuch as the French Revolution, in enshrining that word, in effect committed **parricide.**

parsimonious (adjective) *Excessively frugal.*

Eisenhower, as a young lieutenant, had had to train American soldiers using brooms as facsimiles for rifles, so **parsimonious** had the American isolationist Congress been toward the army.

partita (noun) *A set of musical variations.*

Rosalyn Tureck tells me that the note I sent her, likening Bach's E-minor **Partita** to *King Lear* was right on, that she had played the **partita** a thousand times, but always treated it with awe because she could not know what it would say to her this time around, even as *Lear* cannot be tuned by stroboscope.

patently (adverb) *Obviously; manifestly; plainly.*

Kirov plied Tamayo with questions of theoretical concern to students of Marxism–Leninism and, **patently,** of immediate concern to him.

paternalistic (adjective) *Relating to the practices of a government that undertakes to supply the needs or regulate the conduct of the governed in matters affecting them as individuals as well as in their relations to the state and to each other.*

The inflation that comes inevitably with government pump-priming soon catches up with the laborer, setting off a new deflationary spiral which can in turn only be counteracted by more coercive and **paternalistic** government policies.

patrology (noun) *The study of the source of a discipline, most commonly, the fathers of the Christian faith.*

Here is a man [Cardinal Arns of São Paulo] who studied literature at the Sorbonne, where he achieved his doctorate; who taught **patrology** and didactics at highly respected universities; who has written twenty-five books, including abstruse treatises on medieval literature.

paucity (noun) *Smallness of quantity; dearth, scarcity.*

His subordinates complained with good and ill humor about everything, about the weather, the food, the hygienic facilities, the **paucity** of air cover, the stubbornness of Montgomery, the tenacity of the Germans.

pedagogical (adjective) *Characteristic of teaching.*

Borges: I tried to teach my students not literature but the *love* of literature. I have taught many people the love of Old English.

WFB: And so there is a **pedagogical** art? It isn't simply a matter of—of exposure—you are indoctrinating your students?

pejorative (noun) *A term negative or critical in inclination.*

The term appeaser is used here not merely as a lazy **pejorative.** The appeaser tends to oppose a national draft, to oppose any increase in defense spending, to oppose economic boycotts, cultural boycotts, boycotts of athletic events.

penchant (noun) *Tendency; inclination; liking for.*

George McGovern is a formidable opponent, a crowd-pleaser with a populist-analytical **penchant** that has carried him a long way, though when he ran for President, he was rejected by forty-nine states.

penumbral (adjective) *Shadowy; done under the cover of darkness; concealed.*

Consuelo had engaged in interesting enterprises, most of them concerning Mexicans, often Mexicans seeking ways, legal and **penumbral,** of taking out of Mexico sums of money accumulated by political activity.

penury (noun) *Extreme poverty.*

In some measure, the educator is fortified by the knowledge that despite the trials and **penury** of his existence, he is shaping, more directly than members of any other profession, the destiny of the world.

perdurable (adjective) *Lasting a long time or indefinitely.*

It tends to be true that in England the Establishment prevails. The English Establishment mediates the popular political will through **perdurable** English institutions.

peregrination (noun) *A voyage from place to place to place; voyaging about, especially including foreign countries.*

Conceivably one could find life on Mars—nice old ladies and gentlemen who could tell us that Jesus Christ was a planetary figure of parochial dimension, and by doing so spare the Christian world the awful overhead of all those priests, and nuns, and papal **peregrinations,** and missions, and cemeteries.

peremptory (adjective) *Expressive of urgency or command; of an arrogant or imperious nature.*

Mayday moved forward and put her lips on Blackford's—and lingered. Before she was done, Alice felt contrition over her **peremptory** handling of Anthony, and now used lips and hands to express her feeling for him.

perfervid (adjective) *Excessively, unbalancedly ardent.*

If what the optimists are saying is that a wave of reason is sweeping over the world, how do we account for the **perfervid** worship of the Ayatollah Khomeini the day he was buried?

perfidious (adjective) *Characterized by a deliberate breach of faith, a calculated violation of trust, or treachery.*

"It's your call, Boris. What did bring you out tonight? We have not spoken once in the three years—"

"In the three years in which I have kept pace with your **perfidious** activities, Mr. Chestnut," replied Bolgin.

perfidy (noun) *Deceit; treachery.*

Any effort to pursue an investigation into allegations that the plane that brought down in flames Pakistan leader Zia was sabotaged by sophisticated Soviet chemical explosives was blocked. By the Soviets?

No no no, you don't understand. By the United States. Why expose Soviet **perfidy** when détente is at an exhilarating boil?

periphrastic (adjective) *Ornately long-winded; given to profuse formulations.*

Three cheers for Senator Jesse Helms. As ever, he tends to get to the point of a difficult question with carrier-pigeon directness, leaving many of his sophisticated critics lost in **periphrastic** meaninglessness.

peroration (noun) *The closing part of a speech.*

After the debate was over I shook McGovern's hand and whispered to him, "George, that **peroration** is as good as when I first heard you use it at Dartmouth in 1957." "Yes," he agreed. "Very effective, isn't it?"

perquisites (noun) *Those advantages in a job or in a position that aren't a part of your formal contract.*

Perhaps she was simply doing a job, a job that not only paid well but gave her important **perquisites** in Castro's Cuba—access, for instance, to Diplotiendas, where the select few could buy coffee and extra-conventional luxuries, such as a bar of scented soap imported from Canada, or a chocolate bar.

perspicacious (adjective) *Analytically or visually acute.*

Up until a few years ago, Paris did not permit anyone to publish or to sell the works of the Marquis de Sade. Simone de Beauvoir wrote a book on de Sade in which she stressed the historical and **perspicacious** passages in de Sade, to which the appropriate comment is, "Aha."

pertinacity (noun) *Unyielding persistence, often annoyingly perverse; stubborn inflexibility.*

Blackford muttered something about the **pertinacity** of the press.

pettifoggery (noun) *Little-mindedness; bureaucratic absorption with silly little details.*

To tell the members of the federal judiciary that they cannot get a raise even sufficient to cope with inflation is **pettifoggery** of an ignoble sort.

phantasmagoria (noun) *An ongoing vision, nightmare, fantasy.*

The Chinese Communists are not likely to renounce their **phantasmagoria** explicitly, nor to sacrifice what they call socialist centrism.

philistinism (noun) *The attitudes, beliefs, and conduct characteristic of a crass, prosaic, often priggish individual guided by material rather than intellectual values.*

To paraphrase Mr. Tynan, over here we have the impression that in America everybody thinks alike, that the country is in the grip of an iron **philistinism.**

phlegmatic (adjective) *Slow, stolid, unexcitable.*

"Frankly," said Black at dinner, to his aunt and her **phlegmatic** ever-silent husband, "the idea of going to school in England gives me the creeps."

phlogistonic (adjective) *Heat-producing; combustible.*

Far from demanding with increasing truculence the diplomatic reincorporation of Taiwan, the government of Deng simply let the **phlogistonic** question cool.

pianissimo (adverb; It.) *Very softly.*

Rufus's intensest emotions, like J. S. Bach's, were rendered *pianissimo.*

piquancy (noun) *Something attractively offbeat; provocative.*

M'Lou could always make Sally laugh—that had never been a problem. Sally reacted instantly to humor, as to **piquancy.**

piquant (adjective) *Something attractively offbeat; provocative.*

I was amused that Alan Dershowitz revealed on the program that he himself had never seen the movie *Deep Throat.* That was a **piquant** touch: it enabled him to say, in effect, "I am defending a man for taking part in a movie. What is in that movie is so irrelevant to the defense I shall not even bother to view it."

plainspoken (adjective) *Frank, straightforward, unadorned.*

Normally, when recruiting someone into the Party, the seniority of the recruiter is utterly **plainspoken.** Her authority rested in her established status as a party member; as a graduate of the University of Moscow; as a linguist; as a longtime resident of the Soviet Union.

platonic (adjective) *Tending toward the theoretical or ideal.*

The **platonic** ideal of the unbiased juror presumes a quarrel in which there hasn't been significant national involvement.

plebiscite (noun) *A submission of a proposed new law, or whatever, for a vote by the people.*

It was a very splashy and moving open letter, signed by 170 writers, actors and artists, urging Fidel Castro to hold a **plebiscite** on his rule.

plenipotentiary (noun) *A person invested with full power to transact any business.*

Caroline drew closer to Perry. "I wish you were my minister **plenipotentiary.** I would trust you to do all these things for me, and then if anything at all went wrong, all I would have to do is simply behead you."

plight (verb) *To put or give in pledge.*

One eulogist said that as a young woman, graduated from Vassar College and the Columbia Law School, she had **plighted** her professional troth to two causes: the first, her own individual freedom to do as she chose; the second, her absolute commitment to women's "reproductive rights."

plutocratic (adjective) *Relating to government by the wealthy; of the rule or dominion of wealth or of the rich.*

I very much wish that the meaning of the word "masses" was not so fixed in the Anglo-Saxon world because the word as we use it has either Marxist or **plutocratic** connotations.

polarization (noun) *Division (as of groups, ideologies, systems, or forces) into two opposites.*

The occasion drove home the infinitely sad **polarization** between the Choicers and the Lifers.

polemical (adjective) *Argumentative; intending to make a point at variance with that of your opponent.*

Clare Boothe Luce always had an answer to any question at the tip of her tongue. Though this, I came to know, was **polemical** training; she was often dissatisfied, after consulting her private intellectual conscience, with the answer she gave.

polemicize (verb) *To engage in controversy; dispute aggressively.*

Give me the right to spend my dollars as I see fit—to devote them to learning, to taking pleasure, to **polemicizing,** and if I must make the choice, I will surrender you my political franchise in trade.

polity (noun) *Political organization.*

Some libertarians will never agree that a responsibility of the **polity** is to encourage virtue directly, through such disciplines as service in the militia, reverence for religious values, and jury service.

polyglot (noun) *Someone who speaks or writes several languages.*

If you can speak Spanish that easily, he persists, surely you can run through my book in French? **Polyglots** are that way, I find. They reach a point where every language silts up into a more or less recognizable vernacular.

pomposity (noun) *Ornately showy or pretentiously dignified demeanor, speech, or action.*

Anthony, though formal of speech, was incapable of **pomposity**. He cared more about effective relief for those who suffered than about bombastic relief for those who formed committees.

portentous (adjective) *Exhibiting gravity or ponderousness; self-consciously weighty.*

"What matters is the nature of the Commonwealth."

"I have ideas about that," Caroline said. This sounded **portentous** so she added, "Everybody does . . ."

posit (verb) *To set in place or position; situate; to set down or assume as fact; postulate.*

I **posit** in this case that he is absolutely ignorant of malfeasance. I do this as a matter of character judgment.

positivist (adjective) *Relating to the theory that rejects theology and metaphysics as being merely earlier imperfect modes of knowledge and instead holds that positive knowledge is based on natural phenomena and their properties and relations as verified by the empirical sciences.*

How much harm does *Playboy* do in fact, I have often asked myself, never getting much further than the presumptive disapproval of it, which I extend to any publication that declines to accept extra-personal or extra-**positivist** norms.

postprandial (adjective) *Occurring after a meal, especially after dinner.*

Sitting in the little drawing room of the Moscow apartment, Boris explained to his wife why they must retreat here for any intimate discussions, and routinely after dinner, when, he knew, the **postprandial** relaxation loosens the tongue.

postulate (noun) *A proposition advanced as axiomatic; an essential presupposition, condition, or premise; an underlying hypothesis or assumption.*

When scholars and statesmen disagreed on how to reconcile the **postulates** of America with the survival of slavery, it was to the Declaration of Independence that the abolitionists ideally repaired for guidance. Because the Declaration of Independence spoke of "self-evident" truths. Among them that men are born equal.

Potemkin (adjective) *(Referring to the Russian statesman who built fake villages along a route taken by Catherine the Great) Relating to creating an imposing façade or display designed to obscure or shield an unimposing or undesirable fact or condition.*

There is a little bit too much of the **Potemkin**-tour in the visit of some of the committees to the university. Appointments are set up for them, and they are put in touch with administration and faculty stalwarts.

praepostor (noun) *A monitor at an English public school.*

As **praepostor** at the British public school it had fallen to Anthony Trust to help hold down young Blackford, age fifteen, over one end of a sofa as he received a serious flogging from the headmaster.

pragmatism (noun) *An American movement in philosophy founded by Peirce and James and marked by the doctrines that the meaning of conceptions is to be sought in their practical bearings, that the function of thought is as a guide to action, and that the truth is preeminently to be tested by the practical consequences of belief.*

Brief reference should be made to the substantial contribution to secularism that is being made at Yale and elsewhere by widespread academic reliance on relativism, **pragmatism,** and utilitarianism.

precocity (noun) *Early intellectual or artistic development.*

She walked over to her slender neighbor, whose lined face suggested an age greater than the sixty-one she acknowledged when making one of her frequent references to the **precocity** of her important son.

prefecture (noun) *The office, position, jurisdiction, or term of office of a prefect.*

Though a prefect, Anthony was never a member of the **prefecture.**

prehensile (adjective) *Clutching greedily.*

Later that night, in Sally's car, they made love for the last time under the shadow of the West Rock. She was silent, but **prehensile.**

pre-infanticide (noun) *Killing of a child prior to its birth.*

But to defend the reproductive rights, so-called, of women, it is absolutely necessary to celebrate the act of **pre-infanticide,** and this is not easy for fellow Americans to do.

preponderant (adjective) *Having superior weight, force, or influence; having greater prevalence.*

This means many things, among them that no economic reform that would get in the way of channeling the **preponderant** economic machinery of the country can be tolerated.

preponderate (verb) *To exceed in power, influence, or importance.*

It is well known that in certain quarters in the South where blacks heavily **preponderate,** the marginal black voter (the man whose vote would tip the scales in favor of the Negro block) is, by one evasion or another, deprived of the vote.

prepossession (noun) *An attitude, belief, or impression formed beforehand; a preconceived opinion.*

In the hands of a skillful indoctrinator, the average student not only thinks what the indoctrinator wants him to think (assuming no **prepossession** in the way), but is altogether positive that he has arrived at his position by independent intellectual exertion.

prescience (noun) *The faculty of being able to see ahead.*

We are talking on the eve of near-universal access to the atom bomb. There is little doubt but that the Iraqis would now have it, save for the boldness and **prescience** of the Israelis.

prescind (verb) *To pull out; abstract; disengage.*

[Speaking to Fox Butterfield] On this matter of the economic improvement of the average Chinese life, may I ask, have you found that there is

a considerable tendency to **prescind** from the passage of time improvements in literacy or in health or in food consumption?

presumptive (adjective) *Apparent, presumed; based on inference.*

"This is a pretty good job," the Queen remarked. "I have inherited a lot of money, and a lot of junk, and a lot of perquisites, but there is something in it for everybody because of the **presumptive** necessity to worship something—somebody—worldly."

preternaturally (adverb) *Extremely; more than one would think natural.*

In less than fifteen minutes, Blackford felt **preternaturally** at home with the young Cuban designated by Rufus to be his right hand.

prevarication (noun) *A statement that deviates from or perverts the truth.*

Schlesinger dismissed the **prevarication** as part of the cover story, and confessed that he had not formulated an absolutely satisfactory ethic on the matter of lying to the press.

priapic (adjective) *Preoccupied with or employing the phallus symbolically; featuring or stressing the phallus.*

"At first I thought that his rushing off to see her so often was simply the **priapic** imperative at work."

primogenitive (adjective) *Of or pertaining to the firstborn.*

The English Establishment is more frozen than our own, primarily because theirs is a society based on class. Their Establishment has rites and honorifics and **primogenitive** continuities.

probative (adjective) *Serving to prove; substantiating.*

With Presidents one proceeds more cautiously, because it is not the business of friends, let alone subordinates, to quiz the President. In the first place, one simply doesn't. In the second, a skillful politician could turn away the question easily; and the interrogator gets no **probative** satisfaction.

probity (noun) *Uncompromising adherence to the highest principles and ideals; unimpeachable integrity.*

If the educational overseer is interested in the activity of scholarship, let him endow a research center (and let him not, as a man of intelligence and **probity,** stipulate what shall be the findings of research not yet undertaken).

pro bono publico (adverb; Lat.) *For the public good.*

Paul Hughes was prepared, ***pro bono publico,*** to report secretly to the editors of the *Democratic Digest* the secret doings of the Sub-Committee on Investigations.

proclivity (noun) *An inclination; propensity; leaning.*

One thinks again of Jean-François Revel and his indictment—the **proclivity** of democracies to dissipate energies out of a sense of guilt.

Procrusteanize (verb) *To produce conformity by ruthless means. After Procrustes, a mythical Greek giant, who stretched or shortened captives to make them fit his beds exactly.*

Firing Line does not **Procrusteanize** a guest's formal vocabulary.

prodigality (noun) *Extravagance; reckless spending.*

Newt Gingrich had warmed up on Tip O'Neill, whose genial **prodigality** with the people's purse was accepted as the good-old-boy way of doing things.

prodigy (noun) *An extraordinary, marvelous, or unusual accomplishment, deed, instance, or person.*

Crosstown traffic is bad, but a new traffic commissioner who performed **prodigies** in Baltimore is now in charge.

profanation (noun) *Debasement or vulgarization, especially by misuse or disclosure.*

It is a **profanation** to advance on Kempton's thought with compass, scissors, and tape measure, and it is a sign of his special genius that he inevitably leaves his critics feeling like Philistines.

proffer (verb) *To offer; tender.*

"You are the most exciting, and the most handsome, young physicist in the world. Everybody knows that. What they don't know is that you are also the greatest lover in—in—"

"The spy world?" Alistair Fleetwood **proffered,** laughing.

progenitive (adjective) *Pertaining to those who beget; as in parents, founders, discoverers.*

The proposition that American citizens owe something to the community that formulated and fought to establish their **progenitive** rights was proffered in 1910 by William James, "The Moral Equivalent of War."

promulgate (verb) *To issue a new law or regulation.*

When Rolando Cubela concluded that he had the mandate—to execute Fidel Castro—he was prepared to be ever so cautious in his plans. Nothing reckless. After a month's deliberation, Cubela had it down on paper—in his mind:

1) Castro's death—it must be absolutely assured.

2) A plausible new Cuban government—instantly **promulgated.**

propensity (noun) *Natural inclination; innate or inherent tendency.*

An economic justification for a redistribution of income is the Keynesian insistence that more money go to that group which has a higher **propensity** to consume, that is, the lower and middle income groups.

propitiate (verb) *To appease, conciliate.*

Last Sunday's (London) *Times* reveals that the publishers Viking Penguin, who bought Mr. Rushdie's novel, are negotiating with Britain's Moslem leaders. The objective is to **propitiate** them, and to get from them some sort of peace offering that can be waved across the Mediterranean to the Moslem world.

propitious (adjective) *Presenting favorable circumstances; auspicious.*

With great solemnity, Alistair had been presented the Order of Lenin. Beria explained, "We left out your name—the space is there for it. Security. When the climate is **propitious,** you may take it to a jeweler and have your name inscribed."

proprietary (adjective) *Having to do with the owner; befitting an owner.*

My gal Sal, he had referred to her a few letters back, intending to be affectionate. She had replied, "My gal Sal is entirely too **proprietary** for my taste, Blacky my boy (and how do you like 'Blacky my boy'?)."

prosaic (adjective) *Having a dull, flat, unimaginative quality of style or expression.*

I gathered from my own representative that Lindsay's press conferences tended to be **prosaic** affairs, repetitious, formalistic, called for purely personal exposure.

proscriptively (adverb) *In a prohibiting, interdicting, or proscribing manner.*

The persecution at Harvard of Professor Stephan Thernstrom was for the sin of talking about Jim Crow and about slavery in the South descriptively, rather than **proscriptively** . . .

proselytize (verb) *To convert from one religion, opinion, or party to another; to evangelize.*

Mr. Lovett teaches the Historical and Literary Aspects of the Old Testament, but he does not **proselytize** the Christian faith or teach religion at all.

prosody (noun) *A method or style of versification.*

To pray during the gymnastic exercise of the modern mass, athwart a vernacular **prosody** that belongs in the Chamber of Literary Horrors, is an exercise in self-discipline achieved most easily by the blind and the deaf.

pro tanto (adverb; Lat.) *To a certain extent; proportionately; commensurately.*

Communities blockwide or greater will be given *pro tanto* relief in their property taxes, sufficient to pay the local police bills.

protégé (noun) *A person whose welfare, training, or career is promoted by someone, usually influential or efficient or both.*

By the time Alice Goodyear Corbett had graduated from secondary school she had achieved a minor eminence in the student world of Moscow: the perfectly trained Soviet **protégé.**

provenance (noun) *Place of origin.*

There was just the trace of an accent there, and Blackford could not guess its **provenance,** and of course would not have presumed to inquire.

provincial (adjective) *Limited in scope; narrow, sectional.*

Mr. John Crosby writes: "How do you get on a blacklist? Well, some actors have got on by having foreign names." Tacit premise: blacklisters are reckless, **provincial,** xenophobic.

provincialism (noun) *A narrow, usually uneducated, concern for what lies immediately about you, as distinguished from farseeing, urban, cosmopolitan.*

It isn't a sign of **provincialism** to say that it makes more sense to spend excess dollars on developing domestic fuel options than on inquiring into the flora and fauna of Mars.

proximate (adjective) *Pertaining to the immediately preceding event, or push, or causative factor.*

It is not to give in to economic determinism to reflect on the **proximate** pressures bringing about these reforms in South Africa.

prurient (adjective) *That which seeks out sexual stimulation.*

In 1972, when Harry Reems made *Deep Throat*, the courts were being guided by the Roth standard. That decision, handed down by Justice Brennan in 1957, held that something was obscene if it appealed exclusively to the **prurient** interest and had no "redeeming social importance."

psephologist (noun) *Someone who pursues the scientific study of elections.*

I announce that the **psephologists** have just completed a study that reveals that the participation of Princeton volunteers was the very thing that brought brother Jim (newly elected junior senator for New York) over the edge of victory.

puerile (adjective) *Childish.*

A young man was once a guest of *Firing Line* for the sole reason that he had become, at age twenty-seven or thereabouts, the de facto manager of the mind and body of Bertrand Russell. Here was this **puerile** ideologue sending out invitations in Lord Russell's name to statesmen and scholars the world over to attend a War Crimes Trial of Americans for pursuing an objective in Vietnam, quoting Lord Russell to the effect that there were no differences between the United States and the Nazis.

pulchritude (noun) *Physical comeliness; beauty.*

"Why Baltimore indeed! First, some of the best beer on the East Coast is made here. Second, much of the best seafood in the East is found here. Third, there is **pulchritude** at hand here."

pullulate (verb) *To sprout out; germinate; breed quickly; spring up in abundance.*

But only 1.5 percent of black police officers pass the New York sergeants' test: and the result is a failure of effective social integration, and a them-

and-us attitude which now and again **pullulates** into such incidents as we saw in Los Angeles.

punctilio (noun) *The concern for form, manners, appearance.*

The story of the Bay of Pigs is told again and again. But always in the telling of it, by modern chroniclers, one tends to lose sight of the bloody landscape, so distracted are we by democratic **punctilio.**

pundit (noun) *A wise man, but often used sarcastically. Columnists, for instance, are regularly referred to as "pundits" who "opine"—usually by people who disagree with their punditry.*

Now while George Bush is President, no subordinate is going to come out in favor of legalizing the sale of drugs, the culture shock being as it is. Such proposals are here and there made by a **pundit,** or a mad libertarian, or a fatalist.

purposive (adjective) *Tending to fulfill a conscious purpose or design.*

Individual rights of the sort that for generations were never supposed to be prey to government actions are cheerily disposed of as unjustifiable impedimenta in the way of **purposive** and enlightened state policies.

putative (adjective) *Supposed; ostensible; reputed.*

Much will happen in the weeks and months ahead in conference between the Senate and the House of Representatives, and Senator Helms would be well counseled to exclude from his proscription any **putative** work of art more than fifty years old. This would distinguish the Rodins from the Mapplethorpes.

putatively (adverb) *Supposedly; ostensibly; reputedly.*

It didn't surprise Sally that Art was talking not to old friends, **putatively** interested in Art Shaeffer, football tactician, but to undergraduates he had never met before.

putsch (noun) *A secretly plotted and suddenly executed attempt to overthrow a government or governing body.*

Mr. Adam Clayton Powell, Jr., would be objectionable as a leader whether he became leader following a city-wide **putsch,** or whether he became leader having got one hundred percent of the vote of his constituency.

Q

qua (preposition) *In the character, role, or capacity of; as.*

The Republicans were increasingly maneuvered into the position of believing in John Lindsay *qua* John Lindsay, as their shriveled justification for their original enthusiasm gave way under the weight of one after another entanglement with the same old crowd.

querencia (noun; Sp.) *An area in the arena taken by the bull because he feels safe there.*

Dulles stared at him silently, then turned to talk with Griswold. Black eased away toward Sally—his *querencia,* his love—to lick his wounds.

quietus (noun) *An end; the death of.*

The ABM treaty put a **quietus** on U.S. defensive technology: We even dismantled a protective ring of antinuclear defense missiles planted in the area of Wyoming, and did not trouble to avail ourselves of the option to construct a ring of defensive weapons around Washington, D.C.

quintessence (noun) *The essence of; a pure, typical form of.*

The editor of *Vogue* invited me to explain, explicitly, the "American look" since so many reviewers had denominated Blackford Oakes as being "quintessentially" American. I thought to reject the invitation, because I reject the very notion of **quintessence** as here applied.

quixotic (adjective) *Idealistic and impractical. The word comes from Don Quixote, who tilted at windmills, fancying them an enemy overcome.*

Haydée Santamaría was the sister of the brave man tortured to death during the Moncado fiasco of 1953, when Castro led the **quixotic** charge against the well-fortified barracks at Santiago de Cuba.

quizzically (adverb) *In a slightly and amusingly eccentric manner; questioningly; curiously.*

Alphonse smiled, and bowed his head. "I feel in a bargaining mood, Mr. Oakes." Blackford looked up sharply, **quizzically.**

"I will do as you say," said Alphonse, "provided you give me another drink of vodka."

quotidian (adjective) *Recurring daily.*

I introduced candidate Ronald Reagan in January 1980 with a view to provoking his critics. And I toyed, with the advocate's delight, with the **quotidian** criticisms of Mr. Reagan.

R

Rabelaisian (adjective) *Marked by gross, robust humor, extravagance of caricature, or bold naturalism.*

I remember the old "Truth or Consequences" game they used to play over the radio, which towards the end was coming up with consequences so extravagant as to satisfy **Rabelaisian** appetites for the absurd.

raffish (adjective) *Vulgar; showy.*

Maria wandered over to the entertainment district and was not entirely surprised to find herself talking with a **raffish** man who in his plushily upholstered office looked at her carefully, asked her matter-of-factly to disrobe, examined her again, focused lights on her from various angles, and agreed to employ her.

raillery (noun) *Good-natured ridicule; pleasantry touched with satire; banter, chaffing, mockery.*

I note that the Eighties are held up for scorn and **raillery** by trendy opinion-makers. Everything that came out of the Eighties is held to be somehow contaminated, the grand contaminator being, of course, Ronald Reagan.

rapacious (adjective) *Greedy; ravenous.*

Tom Wolfe records the **rapacious** success of the Bauhaus school, which within a generation had captured almost the whole of the American architectural academy, bequeathing us such megatonnage as, say, the World Trade Center.

ratiocination (noun) *Systematic thought.*

It has occurred to me (after modest **ratiocination**) that style is, really, a matter of timing.

recidivist (adjective) *Of the kind committed before; back to the old business.*

Prisons are bursting at the seams, with over 200,000 more criminals inhabiting quarters than our prisons were designed for, resulting in a

recidivist

gruesome intensification of the awful experience in prison and a resulting increase in **recidivist** crime.

recision (noun) *The act of rescinding or canceling.*

Former Secretary of Defense Caspar Weinberger was in favor of **recision,** but somehow President Reagan never got around to it, in part because it had become a kind of liberal sanctuary, to which disarmament fetishists took pilgrimages every few days, sowing seeds of alarm that suggested that to amend the ABM Treaty was to say good-bye to disarmament.

recondite (adjective) *Very difficult to understand and beyond the reach of ordinary comprehension and knowledge.*

There is a luxurious offering at Yale of courses in the **recondite** byways of human knowledge, wonderful to behold.

rectilinear (adjective) *Moving in a straight line; having an undeviating direction; forming a straight line.*

What gets in the way of **rectilinear** moral reasoning is our insistence on dressing up the moral arguments in opportunistic ways.

rectitude (noun) *Uprightness; righteousness.*

Taiwan was even denied its athletes' participation in the Olympics in Canada, a seizure of diplomatic **rectitude** that did not affect Prime Minister Pierre Trudeau at the expense of any Soviet satellite, though Russia's de facto rule over the Baltic states is at least as questionable—or at least as offensive—as Taiwan's dream of ruling over China.

redoubt (noun) *A small, defensive, secure place; stronghold.*

At places like Harvard, Yale, and Princeton lecturers run into difficulty, because these colleges are not accustomed to paying their speakers the commercial rates; and speakers tend to indulge them, in part out of tradition, in part out of a curiosity to have a look at what used to be the **redoubts** of social and intellectual patricians.

reductio ad absurdum (noun; Lat.) *Reduction to the absurd.*

But perhaps the example is a ***reductio ad absurdum:*** If the United States had a first-strike force, the Soviet Union would presumably fear that it might be used, never mind that during the twenty-odd years when we did have a first-strike force we did not use it.

refectory (noun) *Eating quarters, usually of religious orders.*

The room across the courtyard from the entrance, on the second floor, above what used to be the chapel and was now the printing office from which Castro's instructions flowed out to his subjects, had been the monks' **refectory.**

refractory (adjective) *Resisting control or authority.*

It is easier to deal with **refractory** twelve-year-olds than with eighteen-year-olds. Young children are not consulted on the question of whether they should take instruction.

regicide (noun) *The killing or murder of a king.*

After the original *World-Telegram* story charging vandalism, rape, and **regicide,** the Conservative Party took the precaution of instructing its captains to telephone to inquire whether any complaints had actually been lodged.

regnant (adjective) *The predominating meaning, figure, concept.*

"Are you against labor unions?" an indignant Harriet Pilpel asked Professor Thomas Sowell on *Firing Line.*

Professor Sowell replied, "You asked what were some of the factors that stood in the way of black economic progress and I said that one of them was the labor union. That is a fact, and I'm simply reporting facts, not prejudices." How do you handle such a man, if your political career is staked out on the **regnant** cliché?

reifiable (adjective) *Convertible into something concrete.*

It is in the nature of natural law that it is not fully comprehensible, let alone **reifiable.** What a belief in the natural law actually amounts to is a propensity to do the right thing.

reification (noun) *The conversion of something abstract into something concrete.*

A gesture of recognition—of Martin Luther King's courage, of the galvanizing quality of a rhetoric that sought out a **reification** of the dream of brotherhood—is consistent with the ideals of the country, and a salute to a race of people greatly oppressed during much of U.S. history.

reinstitutionalize (verb) *To incorporate again into a system of organized and often highly formalized belief, practice, or acceptance.*

Gorbachev, who only a year ago declared that the Communist Party's monopoly on political power had to end, is now reaching out for means of **reinstitutionalizing** a Communist hegemony.

remonstrate (verb) *To argue rebukingly.*

Blackford knew better than to **remonstrate** on the theme of the Elusive Distinction.

renascent (adjective) *Born again; recrudescent.*

Effective leadership needs to be shown by the bankruptcy judge, who if properly guided buys the long-term prospects for creditors, which are improved by a **renascent** airline rather than by the sale of its nuts and bolts.

replete (adjective) *Well filled or plentifully supplied; gorged.*

As is almost always the case, special pleaders will find in a 25,000-word document **replete** with qualifications, favorite phrases or clauses designed to make their point.

repristinate (verb) *To restore to an original state or condition.*

Wearily he began to undress, first removing the beard in front of the mirror and staring fondly at his **repristinated** face.

requital (noun) *Return or repayment for something; something given in return or compensation.*

By asking our eighteen-year-olds to make sacrifices we are reminding them that they owe a debt. And reminding them that **requital** of a debt is the purest form of acknowledging that debt.

rescind (verb) *To take back; annul, cancel.*

"I've a terrific idea!" said Blackford. "Why don't you kidnap the Queen, hypnotize her, then send her back and have her **rescind** her invitation to me to do the eulogy?"

resonant (adjective) *Having an effect; being heard; being acted on.*

And, finally, that little boot, quiet but **resonant,** that he finally gave to Mikhail Gorbachev was done adroitly, efficiently, with just the right touch of hauteur: "Gorby, you are getting in the way." Mr. Bush is rightly the man of the hour.

restive (adjective) *Inquisitive; tempted to inquiry, defiance.*

The intellectuals of Spain, in hindsight, recognize the inappropriateness of the republic most of them once supported; but they are **restive,** anxious to get on with the job of crafting organic and responsive and durable political mechanisms.

reticulation (noun) *A network; an arrangement of lines resembling a net.*

When a number of colleges and universities were given over to the thousand blooms of the youth revolution, many of the same people who sharpened their teeth on *God and Man at Yale* were preternaturally silent. They feasted on ideological **reticulation.**

revivification (noun) *The rebirth; the invigoration of; the injection of life into.*

The key to stopping the erosion of Eastern's assets under the aegis of the judge who seems to have the power to conduct either an autopsy or a **re-vivification** is, of course, the unions.

ribaldry (noun) *Language characterized by broad, indecent humor.*

Before we knew it, FBI chief J. Edgar Hoover was bugging motels in which Martin Luther King spent the night, which tapes resulted in vocal **ribaldry** not suitable for family cassettes.

riposte (noun) *A bouncy reply; usually provocative.*

Blackford thought back on the agonies of the Brüderschaft, and for a moment said, reverently, nothing by way of **riposte**. This quickly communicated a hint of resistance to her. He got back into his customary role, the succubus of her taunts.

robustly (adverb) *Frankly, openly, vigorously.*

On entering the **robustly** Victorian Fence Club, to which he had been elected as an undergraduate at about the time of Pearl Harbor, Art's spirits quickly revived.

rodomontade (noun) *A vain, exaggerated boast; a bragging speech; empty bluster.*

I teased my brother Jim by sending him, framed, the headline in the *New York Post* the day after the election, "Buckley: 'I AM THE NEW POL-ITICS,' " getting back from him a winced note of pain at this lapidary record of what looked like a lapse into **rodomontade**.

roistering (noun) *Noisy revelry.*

What ensues is an uproar, in part because the tradition of gentility at the University of Virginia is pronounced, and although a certain amount of alcoholic **roistering** is known to go on, the general protocols are that utter discretion is in order.

Rotarian (adjective) *Of or relating to Rotarian societies; hail-fellow-well-met; concerned with social, civic, and workaday matters.*

People continue to tolerate and to patronize schools and colleges and universities which treat their children like half-rational biological mechanisms, whose highest ambition in life is to develop in such fashion as to render glad the **Rotarian** heart in Anywhere, U.S.A.

rotund (adjective) *Rounded, plump.*

Dr. Callard, the retired headmaster of Winchester, invited in to tea the pleasant young solicitor. Dr. Callard, silver-haired, **rotund,** and genial, served the tea and reminisced.

routinization (noun) *Reduction to a prescribed and detailed course of action to be followed regularly.*

She was amusing herself, draining the meeting of the kind of **routinization** which so many of her predecessors had invested it with.

rubric (noun) *The governing license; the sponsoring idea, concept, protocol.*

The business of being tried by your peers, which is the governing **rubric** in these matters, makes you begin to wonder whether there isn't a bearing between finding Colonel North's "peer" and deciding what it is that he is being tried for.

ruminate (verb) *To let the mind dwell on and develop; disport with.*

One **ruminates** on the analysis, the idealism, the inventiveness, the disillusion, the demoralization expressed by Professor Thomas Sowell.

rump (adjective) *Relating to a fragment or remainder; as a parliament, committee, or other group carrying on in the name of the original body after the departure or expulsion of a large number of its members; a small group usually claiming to be representative of a larger whole that arises independently or breaks off from a parent body.*

Mr. Lindsay's Republican Party is a **rump** affair, captive in his and others' hands, no more representative of the body of Republican thought than the Democratic Party in Mississippi is representative of the Democratic Party nationally.

S

sacerdotal (adjective) *Of or relating to priests or priesthood.*

A half hour into the walk, Brother Hildred asked "Leo"—the monks called themselves by their **sacerdotal** names—if he would like to visit the school's physics laboratory.

sacrosanct (adjective) *Most holy or sacred; inviolable.*

Here in England, three thousand miles away from America, Blackford found it a corporate affront that a **sacrosanct** master should feel free to belittle so great a man as Lindbergh.

sagacity (noun) *Wisdom; soundness of judgment.*

Pedrito nodded his head vigorously, in extravagant recognition of her **sagacity,** and they strolled back toward the little knots of Mexican family friends.

salacious (adjective) *Marked by lecherousness or lewdness; lustful.*

The television reporters ask their own questions and always gravitate to the most **salacious** issues of the day, preferably personal.

salient (noun) *The cutting point; the apex of the military formation, or of an argument.*

President Bush has not confronted the massed will of the Soviet government in any crisis. This doesn't mean that such a will won't materialize, and won't present a crisis. The most obvious **salient** here is West Germany.

salutary (adjective) *Effecting or designed to effect an improvement; remedial.*

By age fifteen Rolando had decided he wished to go into an entirely different kind of life—bloody, yes, but bloody-**salutary,** not bloody-destructive.

salvific (adjective) *Having the intent to save or admit to salvation.*

If we undertake a systematic, devoted, evangelical effort to instruct the people of the world that the Soviet Union is animated not by a **salvific** ideology, but by a reactionary desire to kill and torture, intimidate and exploit others, for the benefit of its own recidivist national appetites for imperialism, we will have done, by peaceful means, what is so long overdue.

sanguinary (adjective) *Bloodthirsty, murderous.*

Let us concede that the death squads of San Salvador are composed primarily of sadistic opportunists who, taking cover in the civil war, pursue their acquisitive and **sanguinary** interests relatively unmolested because of the preoccupation of civil authority with that civil war.

saprophytic (adjective) *Obtaining nourishment osmotically from dead matter.*

If the modern politician's invocation of Lincoln is to be taken as other than opportunistic and **saprophytic,** the invoker must describe what it is about Lincoln that he understands to be the quintessential Lincoln.

saraband (noun) *The music of the saraband, a stately court dance of the sev-*

enteenth and eighteenth centuries resembling the minuet and evolved from a quick Spanish dance of oriental origin.

Rosalyn Tureck giggles her aristocratic warm giggle, leans over, and whispers that she will play me the **saraband** she knows I love.

sass (verb) *To talk impudently or disrespectfully to.*

Senator McCarthy is dead, but the mania he illuminated lives on, and even now asserts control over sensible men whenever their ideology is threatened, questioned, or **sassed.**

sate (verb) *To overfill to the point of glutting; cloying.*

What is it that tempers the appetite of Mikhail Gorbachev for bloody expansionism? Answer: There is no evidence that his appetite is tempered, but much evidence that his appetite cannot be **sated** because of what George Bush might call "the economic thing."

satyagraha (noun) *The pressing of a political or moral position through the doctrine of passive disobedience; associated with Gandhi.*

Of course, China is the great melodramatic event of the political decade, practicing the **satyagraha** of Gandhi on a massive scale, with tanks being deployed, not in unison to march against the masses, but pointing at each other, on the eve of what became a great civil war.

satyriasis (noun) *Abnormal or uncontrollable desire by a man for sexual intercourse.*

But Henry VIII enters the history books as an effective monarch, never mind his **satyriasis,** and his inclination to dispose of unsatisfactory wives on the scaffold.

schismatic (noun) *A deviant (usually religious); unlike the heretic, the schismatic still belongs to the old communion, but is separated from its core authority.*

Is Swaggert's deviant lechery characteristic of evangelical Protestantism? Is Khomeini's genocidal search for **schismatics** and blasphemers a correct transcription of the word of Allah? Is an excommunicated Mormon paradoxically an example of the practicing Mormon?

schuss (verb) *To make a straight, high-speed run on skis.*

Ah, the ideological coda, how it afflicts us all! And how paralyzingly sad that someone who can muse over the desirability of converting New York into an independent state should, having climbed to such a peak, **schuss** down the same old slope, when the mountains beckon him on to new, exhilarating runs.

scintilla (noun) *A barely perceptible manifestation; the slightest particle or trace.*

In the two years he had known her, Blackford had never seen in Sally a **scintilla** of curiosity about anything scientific.

sciolism (noun) *Superficial knowledge; a show of learning without substantial foundation.*

I wasn't sure enough of myself on the facts of Roger Bacon's life, so I didn't note down to challenge Clark on the point; and anyway, he who lives off the exposure of **sciolism** will die from the exposure of **sciolism.**

sciolist (noun) *One whose knowledge or learning is superficial; a pretender to scholarship.*

"I don't believe you. You are an unaccomplished fake. An academic **sciolist.**"

sclerosis (noun) *Hardening of the tissue owing to neglect or overburdening; inactivity to the point of sluggishness, owing to years of inattention or bureaucratic overhead.*

Gorbachev hasn't repealed all those accretions of state socialism. To do so would pit him against every Comrade Ulanov who clings to his position of authority. Besides which, the market needs a little time to extrude three generations of compacted **sclerosis.**

sclerotic (adjective) *Hard, indurated, toughened.*

When you meet with Mr. Milken, you meet at the same time with his lawyer and with a couple of aides. The situation is not for that reason **sclerotic.**

scrupulosity (noun) *The quality or state of carefully adhering to ethical standards; overstrict in applying the strictest standards to oneself.*

He would work at home. I begged him to desist from what I had denounced as his sin of **scrupulosity.**

scurrility (noun) *Abusive language usually marked by coarse or indecent wording or innuendo, unjust denigration, or clownish jesting.*

I have seen libelers try to excuse their own **scurrilities** (what a wonderful word!) against me by pleading that I am a public figure, leaving open the question whether what was said about me was said with actual malice.

sectarian (adjective) *Divisively attached to one faction within a church, ideology, or political party.*

"Khrushchev, we are admiring of the Soviet Union, we are grateful for the aid you are giving us to realize our own socialist revolution, but we cannot be conscripted into the ranks of your **sectarian** wars against Mao," Castro declaimed.

secularist (noun) *One who advocates a view of life or of any particular matter based on the premise that religion and religious considerations should be ignored or purposely excluded.*

Best equipped to challenge the **secularists** in the Department of Philosophy is Professor Robert L. Calhoun, an ordained minister vastly respected as a scholar, as a lecturer, and as a man.

seemliness (noun) *The quality or state of conforming to accepted standards of good form or taste; propriety.*

Such Republican judges as there are, are there simply because judicial **seemliness** requires that a second party should be seen, if not heard—if only to provide those comfortable democratic delusions which are formally satisfying.

seine (verb) *To fish out or pluck from the sea.*

The arraignment and the trial were conducted with the care and precision of an Apollo moon launch, and it is questionable whether even Edgar Smith will succeed in **seining** out of the experience reversible error.

seminal (adjective) *Having the character of an originative power, or source; containing or contributing the seeds of later development.*

In order to penetrate the public mind, it was necessary not only to do such **seminal** thinking as was being done by such as Eric Voegelin, it was necessary also to photograph the ideological father figure in just the right light.

sentimentalization (noun) *The act or process of analyzing a problem with exclusive concern for the sentimental dimension.*

The attempt to answer military questions by asking the question, How much do you love the kid over there who just got married, the youngest son of proud and devoted parents, is a **sentimentalization** of important calculations that are necessarily made, so to speak, in cold blood.

sequester (verb) *To set apart; separate for a special purpose; remove, segregate.*
One can be compassionate for the president of the New York Stock Exchange who goes to jail for his greed, and for the rapist who is unable to control his lust. But it is necessary to **sequester** the transgressors, whatever the genealogy of the aberrations.

seriatim (adverb) *In a series; serially.*
A short, bright, engaging review of the day-in-the-life of each of the candidates appeared **seriatim** in *The New Yorker* during October.

shibboleth (noun) *A word or saying characteristically used by the adherents of a party, sect, or belief and usually regarded as empty of real meaning; a commonplace saying or idea; platitude, truism.*
I appear before you as the only candidate for Mayor of New York who has not a word to say in defense of the proposition that New York ought to stay as big as it is, let alone grow bigger. Is there an argument in defense of this **shibboleth**?

sinologist (noun) *A student of Chinese history, culture, language.*
Novelist and **sinologist** Robert Elegant writes: "Regarding the recent controversy about the emperor of Japan, I should like to quote from an interview that he gave to Bernard Krisher of *Newsweek*."

skein (noun) *Something suggesting the twistings and contortions of a loosely coiled length of yarn or thread.*
J. William Fulbright is renowned as a leading American liberal, and as the author of a vast **skein** of international scholarships whose aim is to foster world understanding and tolerance.

slavish (adjective) *Resembling or characteristic of a slave; spineless, submissive.*
Some companies are moving in that direction, but most of them are **slavish** in meeting the demands of executives they want to stick around.

sloth (noun) *Disinclination to action or labor; sluggishness, laziness, idleness, indolence.*

Those who rail against the microcomputer chip do so for the most practical reason: They have not mastered its use. They strive for metaphysical formulations to justify their hidden little secret (**sloth** and fear).

slovenly (adjective) *Lazily slipshod.*

There is indeed a fusion of justice and anti-Communist activity; the redemptions of the tens of millions whom, because of a **slovenly,** cowardly, and unimaginative diplomacy, we turned over to their Communist oppressors.

sojourn (verb) *To stay as a temporary resident.*

In the spring of 1958, shortly before Mr. Truman was due to **sojourn** at Yale University, I wrote to a professor there whose lot it was to spend hours in close quarters with Mr. Truman.

solecism (noun) *A breach of the formal rules, usually of syntax.*

When lunch was served, the rabbinically disguised Oakes, rather than commit any inadvertent dietary **solecism,** ate nothing, and so emerged from the plane, with his false passport, hungry.

solipsism (noun) *The idea that, actually, only you exist.*

Doesn't it strike you as possibly the case that the twentieth century,

solipsism

where the intellectual and romantic odysseys usually begin from your-self and end up with yourself, becomes therefore the age of **solipsism?**

Solomonic (adjective) *Marked by notable wisdom, reasonableness, or discretion, especially under trying circumstances.*

Primakov returned to Moscow and foreign ministry spokesman Vitaly Churkin has given us the **Solomonic** judgment of his superiors.

sommelier (noun) *A waiter in a restaurant who has charge of wines and their service; a wine steward.*

At La Tambourine, the recessed little table was reserved and Toi, the grandfatherly **sommelier,** had their champagne waiting.

somnambulist (noun) *A sleepwalker.*

To the left and right were cell doors with small apertures at eye level. The only sounds were the occasional moans and what sounded like **somnambulists'** soliloquies.

sonorous (adjective) *Marked by excessively heavy, high-flown, grandiloquent, or self-assured effect or style.*

I maintain that **sonorous** pretensions notwithstanding, Yale does subscribe to an orthodoxy: there are limits within which its faculty members must keep their opinions if they wish to be "tolerated."

sophism (noun) *An argument that is correct in form or appearance but is actually invalid.*

At the moment the nation is very much attracted by the **sophism** of Professor Galbraith, namely that we are not as consumers really free, inasmuch as we are pawns of the advertising agencies.

sophistry (noun) *Reasoning that is superficially plausible but actually fallacious.*

The guardians of this sustaining core of civilization have abdicated their responsibility to mankind. And what is more depressing, they have painted their surrender with flamboyant words and systematic **sophistry** in their efforts to persuade us that far better things are really in store for the world by virtue of their inactivity.

soritical (adjective) *Of or relating to an abridged form of stating a series of syllogisms in a series of propositions so arranged that the predicate of each one that precedes forms the subject of each one that follows and the conclusion* *unites the subject of the first proposition with the predicate of the last proposition. For instance: A = B, B = C, C = D, D = E. Therefore, A = E.*

I remember suggesting to Dan Mahoney that I make the **soritical** leap and announce quite frankly that the defeat of Lindsay was an objective of the Conservative Party.

sostenuto (noun) *A movement or passage whose notes are markedly sustained or prolonged.*

They made for a wonderful dialectic, James Burnham's **sostenutos** and Whittaker Chambers's enigmatic descants.

sotto voce (adverb; It.) *Under the breath; in an undertone.*

"Mr. Oakes, this is Mr. Allen Dulles, deputy director of the Central Intelligence Agency." Black shook hands, and then winked mysteriously and asked *sotto voce:* "How's tricks?"

specious (adjective) *Superficially beautiful or attractive or coveted, but not so in reality; apparently right and proper; superficially fair, just, or correct.*

Note well that Professor Kirkland raised no objection to the fact that what later was demonstrated to be a **specious** biological generalization was taught to several generations of students.

splenetic (adjective) *Characterized by morose bad temper, sullen malevolence, or spiteful, peevish anger.*

The war engaged all the **splenetic** instincts of Khomeini, and he urged all Iran's young people to die in the ecstasy of a mission that transcribed God's will.

squalid (adjective) *Squat, dirty, or wretched in appearance.*

The elm trees were budding on Vassar's neat green campus in the **squalid** city on the day the envelope arrived.

Stakhanovite (adjective) *Pertaining to a worker, especially in the U.S.S.R., whose production is consistently above average and who is therefore awarded recognition and special privileges (after Aleksei Stakhanov, Soviet miner whose efforts inspired it in 1935).*

It is now a solid plank of American history that John F. Kennedy, in respect of American mores, was something of a mess: so to speak, a **Stakhanovite** adulterer.

stasis (noun) *A state of static equilibrium among opposing tendencies or forces; quiescence, stagnation.*

No one doubted that he, nineteen-year-old Tucker Montana, had done some heavy rowing against that current of physical **stasis** that kept saying No, you can't get there from here, nature won't permit it.

stentorian (adjective) *Loud; declaratory; emphatic.*

I can hear even now the vibrancy of Norman Thomas's voice and the **stentorian** tones of the preacher denouncing the sinner. . . . His then current crusade was to save Vietnam and the United States Marines from each other.

stricture (noun) *Something that closely restrains or limits.*

I am confident that the scholar who holds her in esteem and the scholar who does not could both make their way into Yale. Does this mean that Yale, true to the **strictures** of academic freedom, is unconcerned about the teacher's values?

strophe (noun) *Any arrangement of lines together as a unit; stanza.*

Almost every Sunday afternoon I would call him and we would talk, at length, discursively, and laugh together, between the **strophes** of his melancholy.

stultification (noun) *The act or process of invalidation; immobilization; being rendered useless.*

In Brazil, inflation brings unemployment, **stultification** and grinding poverty.

stultifying (adjective) *Rendering useless or ineffectual; causing to appear stupid, inconsistent, or ridiculous.*

The relative independence of adjacent Yugoslavia and the relative geographical isolation from Bulgaria argued the military plausibility and the geopolitical excitement of a genuine Western salient in the cold war, instead of the tiresome, enervating, **stultifying** countersalients to which the West had become accustomed.

suasion (noun) *The act or an instance of urging, convincing, or persuading.*

It is important that the college student's choice be his own, for it is all the more valuable to him if there has been no exterior **suasion** on behalf of one or the other protagonist.

sub specie aeternitatis (adverb; Lat.) *Viewed under the aspects of the heavens; in its essential or universal form or nature.*

Political speculation is necessarily framed by the values that contemporary history composes. So that any distinction-making, however relevant *sub specie aeternitatis,* simply ought not to be attempted in addressing, for instance, six thousand policemen three weeks after the horrors of Selma, Alabama.

subsume (verb) *To view, list, or rate as a component in an overall or more comprehensive classification, summation, or synthesis.*

The geopolitical argument in favor of withdrawal is **subsumed** in the moral argument in favor of liberating Iraq from Saddam Hussein.

subterfuge (noun) *A deception.*

"It is inconceivable that Khrushchev should have authorized any such **subterfuge** without—well, without my authorization," Castro said.

succinct (adjective) *Marked by brief and compact expression or by extreme compression and lack of unnecessary words and details.*

The basic story is uncomplicated, though the account of it by Kenneth Tynan in the current *Harper's* is not. That is too bad, in a man who knows how to be **succinct.**

succubus (noun) *An evil spirit, but the victim, or supine partner of, the aggressive incubus.*

Blackford thought back on the agonies of the Brüderschaft, and for a moment said, reverently, nothing by way of riposte. This quickly communicated a hint of resistance to her. He got back into his customary role, the **succubus** of her taunts.

summum bonum (noun; Lat.) *The supreme or highest good, usually in which all other goods are included or from which they are derived.*

Self-rule continues to tyrannize over the liberal ideology, secure in its place as the *summum bonum.*

sunder (verb) *To break or force apart, in two, or off from a whole; separate,* *usually by rending, cutting, or breaking, or by intervening time or space; sever.*

David Lindsay and Jim Buckley became fast friends at Yale, and of all the personal dislodgements of the campaign I am most grievously concerned over the possibility that it may have **sundered** that friendship.

sundry (adjective) *Various; miscellaneous; divers.*

We do not know what would be the cost of rebuilding Kuwait City, and it is of course hard to calculate the damages done by torturers, murderers, rapists, and **sundry** sadists.

superannuation (noun) *Becoming useless, because of age.*

I have mentioned that a study last summer reveals that there is a greater turnover in the House of Lords (from **superannuation**) than there is in the House of Representatives (where 99 percent of the incumbents who ran for office were returned to office last November).

supererogatory (adjective) *Verbally redundant, superfluous.*

[On having been requested to send a seconding letter by the sponsor of Franklin Delano Roosevelt, Jr., to the New York Yacht Club] I would have thought that my own inclinations on the matter of his proposed membership would have been **supererogatory,** or ideologically suspect.

supernal (adjective) *Being or coming from above; that which emanates from heaven.*

On the main highway he stopped, sticking up his thumb with that **supernal** confidence of the young that he would not be kept waiting.

supernumerary (adjective) *Exceeding what is necessary, required, or desired; superfluous.*

Did that auxiliary go on to unemployment? Or might it be that he went on to a higher-paying job? An unanswerable question which challenges the dynamic of a free society to decline to hire someone at a lower wage because by doing so someone being paid a higher wage becomes **supernumerary.**

supine (adjective) *Lying, so to speak helplessly, on one's back; manifesting mental or moral lethargy; indifferent to one's duty or welfare or others' needs.*

No one not apathetic to the value issues of the day can in good con-

science contribute to the ascendancy of ideas he considers destructive of the best in civilization. To do so is to be guilty of **supine** and unthinking fatalism of the sort that is the surest poison of democracy and the final abnegation of man's autonomy.

suppurating (adjective) *Generating pus; giving out poison.*

In Leningrad the successor to Romanov was defeated—even though he ran unopposed—thus documenting the failure of Communism to transform human nature. Now that is an official part of the Soviet record. And nothing *Pravda* can do to bury the results of the vote can hide the **suppurating** sore: Marxist man is a human badly clothed and underfed.

surcease (noun) *Cessation; especially a temporary suspension, intermission, or respite.*

Having got the votes of men and women who, in this city, are unemployable, the politicians let them institutionalize themselves as social derelicts, at liberty to breed children who, suffering from inherited disadvantages, alternatively seek **surcease** in hyperstimulation and in indolence.

surreptitious (adjective) *Hidden; out of sight; clandestine.*

Ingenio Tamayo was a mean-spirited man—who very much enjoyed performing Fidel Castro's highly **surreptitious** commissions primarily because they called for the discreet elimination of someone Castro did not wish officially to detain and execute.

sycophantic (adjective) *The manner of someone who seeks to gain favor by flattery.*

Castro laughed. He laughed uproariously. Such a laugh as demands of subordinates **sycophantic** acquiescence.

syllabus (noun) *A compendium or summary outline of a discourse, treatise, course of study, or examination requirements.*

The final point in Hart's **syllabus** is the most intriguing. He suggests that abusive language can be and often is a form by which general frustrations get expressed by younger people.

syllogism (noun) *An argument or form of reasoning in which two statements or premises are made and a logical conclusion drawn from them; reasoning from the general to the particular; deductive logic.*

What is curious about the proposed reform is that its unwritten language is suggesting: Our senators are for sale for speaking fees. Therefore, we shan't have speaking fees. Therefore our senators will no longer be for sale. The **syllogism** is very leaky.

symbiosis (noun) *The profitable coexistence of two organisms, to their mutual advantage.*

The counsel to President Truman began by advising him that the president had no authority to engage in secret intelligence work in peacetime, but later, under pressure, revised this opinion to the effect that if a president OKs a secret enterprise and Congress provides the funds for carrying it out, the **symbiosis** between these two acts breeds a little constitutional baby, through artificial insemination.

synaesthetic (adjective) *Experiencing a subjective sensation or image that appeals to all the senses.*

All I need do to repay everyone from Bach to the piccolo player is to shell out fifteen or twenty dollars for the music that can realize sublimity for the ear and the mind, if the experience, appealing at once to all the senses, is **synaesthetic.**

synecdoche (noun) *The single example, in place of the whole. The one, for the many.*

Luce: The Old Testament myth of the Garden of Eden has aroused the ire of women feminists for generations. God creates heaven and earth in this legend in Genesis. He then creates man; man shares in the spirit of God.

WFB: Man the male or man the **synecdoche** for human beings?

synergistic (adjective) *Having the capacity to act in cooperative action of discrete agencies such that the total effect is greater than the sum of the two or more effects taken independently.*

Moskos believes we are ready to march together under a **synergistic** banner enjoining us to do everything we can for our country, while our country does everything it can for us.

synoptic (adjective) *Affording a general view of a whole, of what came before.*

In the creation of comic strips, there is the nagging mechanical—and therefore artistic—problem of reintroducing the reader to the **synoptic** point at which he was dropped the day before.

syntactical (adjective) *Relating to the rules of syntax, a connected system of order; orderly arrangement; harmonious adjustment of parts or elements.*

It is a highly regarded national secret that Mr. Eisenhower has a way of easing virtually every subject he touches into a **syntactical** jungle in which every ray of light, every breath of air, is choked out.

T

tabula rasa (noun; Lat.) *The condition of the mind before it is exposed to anything; total innocence, blankness.*

What Judge Gerhard Gesell and the defendants appear to be looking for is Seven Truly Ignorant Washingtonians, who will approach the question

tabula rasa

of Colonel North, guilty or innocent, *tabula rasa*—with absolutely un-
formed opinions.

tacit (adjective) *Implied or indicated but not actually expressed.*
One must hope that the President's **tacit** approval of Dole's Bill was wrung
from him in the middle of a coughing fit, during which Mr. Reagan could
not collect his senses.

taciturn (adjective) *Temperamentally disinclined or reluctant to talk or converse.*
The reporter talked on and on, but my **taciturn** answers finally discour-
aged him; we shook hands and he left.

talismanic (adjective) *Having the properties of something that produces extraordinary or apparently magical or miraculous effects.*
It is a pity that there has developed the **talismanic** view of democracy, as
the indispensable and unassailable solvent of the free and virtuous society.

tangential (adjective) *Deviating widely and sometimes erratically; divergent; touching lightly or in the most tenuous way; incidental.*

Why did Wagner subtly underwrite the distorted newspaper accounts? The necessary answer, barring **tangential** motives of unscientific bearing, is—because to do so made good politics.

tantamount (adjective) *Equivalent in value, significance, or effect.*

In most situations only penny-wise thinking and inherent dishonesty would lead to a prescription by the subsidizer as to the outcome of research. This would be **tantamount** to a cigarette company's granting money for research into cancer, with the stipulation that it shall not be discovered that tobacco is in any way conducive to the spread of the disease.

tautology (noun) *The statement of that which is obvious, and therefore does not need restating; redundancy.*

Now, the fact that six times as many shootings occur in houses that have guns as don't have guns seems to me—well, the **tautology** is, you obviously can't have a shooting where you don't have guns.

taxonomize (verb) *Systematically to distinguish, order, and name type groups within a subject field.*

Now there is of course no set rule by which pork is **taxonomized** as exactly that.

temporize (verb) *To act to suit the time; adapt to a situation; bow to practical necessities.*

We are therefore at one and the same time taking, against Saddam Hussein, a principled line with moral appeal; while, with Gorbachev, we **temporize.**

tendentious (adjective) *Stated in such a way as to promote a cause; not impartial.*

I pause here to remark that the series is politically **tendentious.** It is a plain matter of record that Bobby Kennedy was the man who authorized the taping of Dr. King.

tendentiously (adverb) *Stated in such a way as to promote a cause; not impartial.*

In his opening statement, John Kenneth Galbraith got about as much as one can possibly hope to get from twelve minutes: rapport with the audience; a broad statement of his position, **tendentiously** given; a sense of wisdom and of realism; and a bite or two to show the audience that the speaker has plenty of ginger, and knows just where, as required, to stick it.

tenet (noun) *A principle, dogma, belief, or doctrine generally held to be true; especially one held in common by members of an organization, group, movement, or profession.*

It seems unjust to employ pernicious techniques to undermine the **tenets** of Christianity. Most students are unaffected, but some, impressionable and malleable, lose faith in God.

tergiversation (noun) *Reversal of opinion; backsliding.*

We are laggard on that deterrent front and we face a concrete problem in Europe given the **tergiversation** of Helmut Kohl on the modernizing of the remaining nuclear missiles in West Germany.

theocracy (noun) *Government of a state by theological doctrine.*

But the state (under the Shah) was not run as a **theocracy,** and one wonders therefore exactly what it is that the Ayatollah has in mind when he speaks of an Islamic republic.

thither (adverb) *To or toward that place; in that direction; there.*

Alistair Fleetwood, for the moment confused, pointed vaguely at a corner of the room. **Thither** the porter went.

tocsin (noun) *A bell used to sound an alarm or a general summons.*

Michael Harrington published a book, *The Other America.* The book described a portion of the American population beset by tormenting poverty. Its thesis was brought to the attention of President Kennedy on November 19, 1963. The book sounded the **tocsin** for massive federal action to "make war" on poverty.

toothsome (adjective) *Agreeable, pleasant; abundant.*

He had lived, up until just after his fortieth year, a robust sensual life, in America and in Europe, using up most of the **toothsome** legacy he had been left by his parents.

torpor (noun) *Mental or spiritual sluggishness; apathy; lethargy.*

If the nation is constantly at war, or subject to plagues and starvation, national **torpor** threatens to set in.

tort-feasor (noun) *One who is guilty of a wrongful act; a wrongdoer; a trespasser.*

The relevant questions, after the shooting down of the Korean airliner, were: (1) How does one punish a punishable act? (Answer: By demanding reparations.) (2) How does one take reasonable steps to see to it that such an act is not committed again? (Answer: By getting assurances from the **tort-feasor.**)

totalism (noun) *Exercising total autocratic powers: tending toward monopoly.*

The thoroughly non-Ideological Man is usually designated as steward of the American political community. This is partly a good thing, because everyone knows that ideological **totalism** can bring whole societies down.

totemism (noun) *A system of social organizations based on emblematic affiliations.*

Not a week goes by that we at *National Review* do not need to call a point of order; or fit together the parts to show a current piece of humbuggery; or scrub down someone's shiny new proposal to expose the structure for what it is—usually Liberal **totemism.**

traduce (verb) *To lower or disgrace the reputation of; expose to shame or blame by utterance of falsehood or misrepresentation.*

A hundred organizations would lash out against Yale. They would accuse her of **traducing** education, of violating freedom.

transcendent (adjective) *Going beyond or exceeding usual limits; surpassing; being above material existence or apart from the universe.*

The dissipation of the moral satisfaction earned by Mr. Bush merits careful examination: because it teaches us that rigid geopolitical formulae have to yield, in special circumstances, to moral considerations, when these achieve **transcendent** importance.

transliterate (verb) *To represent or spell (words, letters, or characters of one language) in the letters or characters of another language or alphabet.*

The Japanese use many self-effacing conventions which, **transliterated** into English, are startling to say the least.

transubstantiate (verb) *To change into another substance; transform; transmute.*

Surely a society that has the power to conscript, and in many cases send men to their deaths in defense of that flag and its citizens, has also the right to guard against desecrating the flag that symbolizes, even it if does not **transubstantiate,** their ideals.

travesty (noun) *A debased distortion or imitation or representation; sham, mockery.*

In Venezuela, Pérez Jiménez was boss. He decided to hold an "election" at which all the people, of course, would have the option of "approving" the government of Pérez Jiménez or—well, no one was exactly sure, or what. Indeed, here was a palpable **travesty** on democracy.

treacle (noun) *Something (as a tone of voice, manner, or compliment) resembling treacle, a blend of molasses, invert sugar, and corn syrup, being heavily sweet and cloying.*

Shall we attempt to mulct some meaning out of that **treacle**? He is suggesting that President Reagan was not "determined." And that he was not a "leader." That will not be very easy to establish about a man who when he ran for reelection, garnered the vote of forty-nine states.

tremulous (adjective) *Trembling; quivering; palpitating; timid.*

Never having heard Kirsten Flagstad speak, I can say only that her singing voice was a **tremulous** experience.

trenchant (adjective) *Forceful; tightly constructed.*

Norman Podhoretz was associated with the left in American politics until some time in the late sixties, when he gradually, but with that **trenchant** willpower which even his critics acknowledge, changed his mind. Since then he has been a penetrating critic of disorderly thought and romantic views of the Soviet Union.

trenchantly (adverb) *In a keenly articulate or sharply perceptive manner; cogently.*

The educated man, Russell Kirk has **trenchantly** said, is the man who has come to learn how to apprehend ethical norms by intellectual means.

trinitarian (adjective) *Having three parts; threefold; usually referring to the Christian belief in the Trinity. Opposite of unitarian.*

Now the intricacies of the alleged crime of Salman Rushdie are read for the most part by Westerners for whom discussion of whether the word "prostitute" can conceivably characterize the prophet's wives, or whether the term "Mahmoud" can ever be used to refer to the prophet is about as engaging to Christians and Jews as discussions of the **trinitarian** God of the Christians engage the Moslem world.

tripartite (adjective) *Divided into or being in three parts; composed of three parts or kinds.*

Yes, the Israeli people have lined up for gas masks and are practicing civil defense, as who would not at this moment. But the great drama is **tripartite.**

troglodytic (adjective) *Relating to cave dwellers; dwelling in or involving residence in caves.*

His light suntan belied the **troglodytic** life spent plumbing the mysteries of spooks.

tropism (noun) *An innate tendency to react in a definite manner to stimuli; a natural born inclination.*

Because we know that women should be educated and should vote and should exercise their capacity to lead does not dissipate that **tropism** that assigns to the woman primary responsibility for the care of the child, and to the man, primarily responsibility for the care of the woman.

troth (noun) *One's pledged word.*

We should not have been surprised when the spokesman for Castro carefully explained to us that the **troth** had been plighted by the Cuban people thirty years ago once and for all: In the Marxist world there is no retreat from history.

truculent (adjective) *Combative; vitriolic.*

Firing Line programs have almost always been governed, temperamentally, by the attitude and behavior of the guest. Norman Thomas was a highly **truculent** debater (a running distemper was a part of his public persona).

truculently (adverb) *Belligerently, pugnaciously.*

"What's the matter with that?" Baroody's pipe tilted up **truculently.**

truncated (adjective) *Cut short.*

I try a **truncated** version of the talk I gave the night before, wondering whether I might just discover, in this new version, that it is better communicated short than long.

tumbril (noun) *A vehicle for carrying condemned persons (as, political prisoners during the French Revolution) to a place of execution.*

We're worried as hell over what Stalin is up to. A purge, maybe of classic proportions, is under way. The **tumbrils** are full and, as usual, full of his own past intimates.

tumultuous (adjective) *Violently agitated; uproarious.*

During the **tumultuous** month since being told he would be returning to Cuba on an important mission, he had been given intensive training.

tu quoque (adjective; Lat.) *Referring to a retort charging an adversary with being or doing what he criticizes in others.*

At a meeting with the distinguished editors of a distinguished newspaper, the dark point was explicitly raised, and I knew there was no easy answer, save the old *tu quoque* argument.

turpitude (noun) *Corruption; evildoing; iniquity.*

Neither Ronald Brown nor other victims of Republican **turpitude** specify what it is that Republicans did to Wright that Democrats didn't also do to Wright, given the ethics panel's bipartisan vote.

tutoyer (verb; Fr.) *To address familiarly, from the French* tu *as distinguished from the more formal* vous.

I am, in public situations, disposed to formality. On *Firing Line,* even if I have *tutoyed* them for decades, I always refer to my guests as Mr., Mrs., or Miss So-and-So.

U

ultramontanist (noun) *Pertaining to one who favors greater supremacy of papal over national or diocesan authority in the Roman Catholic Church.*

Sister Elizabeth did not want Manhattanville to be referred to as a "Catholic college." Call Sister Elizabeth, I had asked Aggie Schmidt, an **ultramontanist** graduate of Manhattanville, and tell her we are going to have to discuss the question of Manhattanville's Catholicism on the program, because after all that's the kind of thing the program is about.

ululation (noun) *Howls or wails; cries of lamentation.*

The original idea (Kemp–Roth) was to reduce taxes evenhandedly. Since everyone knows that 10 percent of $100,000.00 is more than 10 percent of $10,000.00, the Reaganites should have been prepared for all that rhetoric about favoring the rich. But not having stressed the risks of excessive progressivity, they proved unready for it. Came then the big media **ululations** about the rich.

uncongruous (adjective) *Not conforming to the circumstances or requirements of a situation; unreasonable, unsuitable.*

A teacher who devotes himself to undermining the premises of the school at which he teaches, or the society in which he lives, may properly be deemed **uncongruous.**

unctuous (adjective) *Revealing or marked by a smug, ingratiating, and false appearance or spirituality.*

I maintain that if you put every politician in New York who appears before you groveling and **unctuous** and prepared to turn the entire apparatus of New York and put it at your disposal on a silver tray—you will not substantially augment the happiness, the security, the sense of accomplishment of your own people.

unmeeching (adjective) *Not cringing, sneaky, or whining in tone.*

Sometimes the politician will want to identify the demon, in which case the accusations are direct in reference and **unmeeching** in tone.

unshirted (adjective) *Undiluted; unsparing; undisguised.*

Charles Murray, Manhattan Institute author of *Losing Ground*, urges President Bush to give **unshirted** hell to the critics of private education.

untenable (adjective) *Unable to be defended or maintained.*

Opposition to the brand of collectivism espoused by Morgan or Tarshis or Samuelson is simply **untenable,** and what little recognition is given to that barely noticeable corps of economists who repudiate the collectivists' program is sometimes forthrightly savage.

urbane (adjective) *Having or showing the refined manners of polite society; elegant, cosmopolitan.*

The aide wrote back to the box number designated. That letter got back an **urbane** letter advising the aide that if the Director was not interested in knowing what the internal fighting within the Kremlin was all about, perhaps the Director should resign his position as head of CIA and become Baseball Commissioner?

usurious (adjective) *Involving charging an unconscionable or exorbitant rate or amount of interest.*

A tricky diplomatic business, but the CAB recognized a responsibility to protect American consumers, and therefore acted favorably on a suit the effect of which could be to deny landing rights to foreign carriers that continued to extort from passengers the **usurious** rate.

usurpation (noun) *The wrongful assumption of power.*

A constitutional amendment, done athwart the will of the Court for the first time in modern history, would accomplish more than simply bringing relief to the majority who consider themselves victims of judicial **usurpation.**

utilitarian (adjective) *Stressing the value of practical over aesthetic qualities; characterized by or aiming at utility as distinguished from beauty or ornament.*

The apartment was appropriately **utilitarian,** as though quickly furnished for a transient client.

V

vacuity (noun) *Emptiness of mind; lack of intelligence, interest, or thought; an inane or senseless thing, remark, or quality.*

Six weeks before he was inaugurated, I lunched privately with Senator Quayle, taking the opportunity to search out that highly advertised **vacuity.** I didn't find it.

vainglorious (adjective) *Marked by ostentation or excessive pride in one's achievements.*

To have mentioned in this book that I had been the co-chairman of an

Inter-Faith Conference would have been irrelevant, perhaps even **vainglorious.**

valedictory (noun) *Farewell; that which is said in the course of ending a speech or bidding good-bye.*

Fidel Castro had never succeeded in expunging from his own or others' use the traditional Cuban **valedictory** that one should go forward with God.

vapid (adjective) *Lacking flavor, zest, animation, or spirit.*

All the questions were the obvious ones, and it gave me a chance to formulate some of those **vapid** responses that are indispensable to the success of a constitutional monarch.

varicose (adjective) *Abnormally swollen or dilated.*

He was habituated now to the redundancy of the Trail's surrounding features—the hanging Spanish moss–like vegetation, the sprouts of sharp underbrush, the **varicose** little ditches engraved by the spring floods.

variegated (adjective) *Varied; especially marked with different colors or tints in spots, streaks, or stripes.*

At twelve I persuaded my indulgent father to give me a boat. The boat was a sixteen-foot Barracuda (a class since extinct), and I joined the **variegated** seven-boat fleet in Lakeville, Connecticut.

vaticination (noun) *A prediction; prophecy.*

[WFB speaking on *Firing Line* with Norman Thomas] Because in point of fact, if you don't mind, rather than simply—automatically—accept your **vaticinations,** I'd like to point out that in Korea, we did actually stop the aggressor.

velleity (noun) *A slight, i.e., nonfervent wish.*

People get annoyed when you use words that do not come trippingly off the tongue of Oprah Winfrey, but how else than to designate it as a **velleity** would you describe President Bush's fair-weather call for landing some people on Mars?

venal (adjective) *Corrupt; susceptible of being bought.*

Here is what the *New York Times* invites the reader to think. Joe Coors is a wealthy brewer from Colorado and is known to be a hot conservative. It is especially ironic under the circumstances that he should be the **venal** influence peddlar.

venial (adjective) *That may be forgiven; pardonable; excused; overlooked.*

It is proper to raise the question whether this is an indication of the dulled morality of the public, or whether the misuse of public transportation is merely a **venial** offense.

verisimilitude (noun) *Authenticity; the appearance of being the genuine article.*

Fidel explained, his voice now conversational, "The repetition? 'A most terrible, a most horrible accident?' As a writer, I would not engage in such crude repetitions. But here, it gives **verisimilitude** to the heat with which I am speaking."

vermiform (adjective) *By derivation, "wormlike"; used almost exclusively to suggest "useless," even as some human organs are thought of as vermiform appendices, e.g., the appendix.*

The other day, historian Arthur Schlesinger, Jr., was lamenting the very institution of vice president, on the grounds that he was not really elected by the people; rather, he is a **vermiform** appendix of the presidential nominee, who comes to life only when the president dies or is shot.

vernacular (noun) *The language spoken in the informal idiom of a trade or profession; informal idiom.*

He reiterated—it had to be a native Soviet. No Cuban, never mind his training in Russian, could master the kind of **vernacular** the Kremlin would expect to receive in telexes from the field, the bureaucratic accretions, the idiomatic twists and turns.

vestigial (adjective) *Remaining or surviving, however degenerate, atrophied, or imperfect.*

When the Poles declared martial law and a country of forty million people found itself without the **vestigial** liberties it had been exercising, there was an outcry.

vexatious (adjective) *Annoying, troublesome.*

On the other hand, to suppose that the latter won't get into **vexatious** troubles is to guess wrong, as witness the matter of Edwin Meese.

vinous (adjective) *Caused by or resulting from drinking wine or spirits; showing the effects of the use of wine.*

Bui Tin once said to him, after a long and **vinous** meal, that Le Duc Sy's mutinous inclinations were really undifferentiated; he had not got on with the Reverend Mother, nor with the principal at their primary school; nor had he really got on with his father.

viscous (adjective) *Having a ropy or glutinous consistency and the quality of sticking or adhering.*

I cannot think as the crow flies for very long, unless I am wrestling with somebody, or something, more **viscous** than my own runny thoughts.

vitiate (verb) *To impair the value or quality of.*

I asked Chiang Ching-kuo, the son of Chiang Kai-shek, whether there was any possibility that Taiwan might make an alliance with the Soviet Union at some point in the future, if necessary to substitute for **vitiating** Western support (President Carter had recently booted CCK's ambassador out of Washington, replacing him with China's).

vitriol (noun) *Virulence of feeling or speech.*

Lyndon Baines Johnson was morose. When that happened, the **vitriol** reigned for the initial period, and then he would focus his powerful mind on the vexation, the irritant, the goddam son of a bitch creating the problem!

volatile (adjective) *Characterized by quick or unexpected changes; not steady or predictable.*

Pyotr Ivanovich was a **volatile** man who felt that genuine emotion cannot be communicated except by totalist vocal measures.

volubly (adverb) *Talkatively.*

Betancourt, who had early on sided enthusiastically with Castro and his insurgency, was by now **volubly** disgusted with what Castro had done to his country.

voluminous (adjective) *Filling or capable of filling a large volume or several volumes; profuse, exorbitant.*

We should face it that understanding the Russians isn't something we are ever likely to master. James Reston struggles valiantly in his column and says perhaps they shot down the Korean airliner because they were invaded by Napoleon. That's as good a guess as any. Even concentrated Soviet-watchers are surprised by the **voluminous** lies being told about the downing of KA flight 007.

voluptuarian (adjective) *Lustful; sensuous.*

Anthony leaned forward, got up to stir the log fire, and sat down again, his face radiant in what, under entirely different circumstances, Blackford had once referred to as "your lewd, **voluptuarian** smile."

voluptuously (adverb) *In a full and appealing manner.*

"Sir Alistair!" He allowed the syllable to pass **voluptuously** through his lips. Until exactly 12:44 that afternoon he had been simply Mr. Alistair Fleetwood.

votary (noun) *A sworn adherent; an ardent enthusiast; a devoted admirer; a disciple, fan.*

A senator might say, "We are going to do everything we can to help the Red Cross," by which he means he, his administrative assistants, his uncles and aunts, friends and **votaries** will jointly do what they all can for the Red Cross.

vox populi (noun; Lat.) *Popular opinion.*

The Inquiring Photographer, a New York City institution which delivers the *vox populi* for the *New York Daily News*, asks questions of the people it interviews, the answers to which are often superficial or wrong-headed.

vulgar (adjective) *Deficient in taste, delicacy, or refinement.*

The four of them shared the living room for a few minutes, after which they separated. And in due course, in that charmingly **vulgar** room, Minerva was soon giggling as "Charles" expressed his affection for her.

vulgarian (noun and adjective) *A person of vulgar habits, mind, manners, dress, or behavior.*

All of this adulation, which reaches even into the demonstrators' square, was for a man (Mao Tse-tung) at once the total **vulgarian;** and the Brobdingnagian dictator, a kind of King Kong poet.

vulgar

W

warrant (verb) *To declare or maintain with little or no fear of being contradicted or belied; be certain; be sure that.*

"The collegers at Eton," said Mr. Alex-Hiller, "there on scholarships are selected from the poorer classes. This is not to say that there are brighter boys among the poor than among the rich."

"No, that doesn't say it, but I **warrant** it's true," said the Queen.

Weltanschauung (noun; Ger.) *One's world-philosophy, the sum of one's essential views (on politics, theology).*

People are curious about the Impossible Guest. I could name but won't the guest whose entire knowledge of life filled eight minutes, so that when the ninth came along, he simply recycled his *Weltanschauung* for the next eight minutes.

whimsical (adjective) *Characterized by a capricious or eccentric idea.*

Smith's prison mates administered a thorough beating to the child-killer. Sure, Smith's companions thought the murder of a fifteen-year-old a repellent form of crime; but these nice discriminations, among men who mug and rape and kill, are **whimsical.** In their eyes, Edgar Smith's crime was that he had confessed guilt to a murder after maintaining his innocence for twenty years.

williwaw (noun) *A gust of cold wind; a mini-gale.*

When the anti-Semitic **williwaw** of the mid-thirties suddenly threatened to grow to Typhonic force, young Astra led her widowed mother to meet her river friend, the elderly policeman with a fondness for the children who played along the river's verdant banks.

winnow (verb) *To separate, seeking the better, or the best; to analyze, with the same purpose in mind.*

When the anti-federalists mobilized during the days the Constitution was being discussed, they enunciated what was to become the Bill of Rights. This list of rights included Provision No. 7 which was both more wordy and more absolute than what **winnowed** down into the Second Amendment.

wreak (verb) *To bring about harm; cause, inflict.*

Most of the analysts reasoned that here was a hard-planned, nationally subsidized, highly organized campaign to **wreak** vengeance on John Lindsay.

Wykehamist (noun) *A student or graduate of Winchester College, England.*

Fleetwood had been attracted to the tall, rangy **Wykehamist** who devoted himself equally to physics, soccer, and politics.

X

xenophobia (noun) *A hatred, fear, or suspicion of that which is foreign, or of foreigners.*

A factor not to be dismissed is the **xenophobia** of a great power (China) that for a century and a half was a plaything of the younger sons of European noblemen.

xenophobia

About the Book

FOR SOME YEARS William F. Buckley Jr., at a publisher's request, has been drawing up his own word lists, and pairing each word with a citation from his published works, somewhat like a one-man French Academy writing his own dictionary. The lists were initiated by the ingenious firm of Andrews & McMeel, which each year publishes a calendar titled *William F. Buckley Jr.'s 365 Words You'd Like to Know*. The words included here in *The Lexicon* are all part of the author's working vocabulary. The books from which they are taken include *Cruising Speed* (G. P. Putnam's Sons, 1971), *God and Man at Yale* (Regnery Books, 1986), *Gratitude* (Random House, 1990), *High Jinx* (Doubleday, 1986), *Mongoose, R.I.P.* (Random House, 1987), *On the Firing Line* (Random House, 1989), *Right Reason* (Doubleday, 1985), *Rumbles Left and Right* (G. P. Putnam's Sons, 1963), *Saving the Queen* (Doubleday, 1976), *Tucker's Last Stand* (Random House, 1990), *The Unmaking of a Mayor* (The Viking Press, 1966), and *Up From Liberalism* (Stein & Day, 1984), as well as William F. Buckley Jr.'s syndicated column "On the Right."

The Lexicon originally appeared in different form as part of the volume *Buckley: The Right Word*, selected and edited by Samuel S. Vaughan, and published in hardcover by Random House in 1996 and in paperback by Harvest Books in 1998.